Coronado's Garage

A Memoir

By Arnoldo X. Cuellar

Contents

Dedication

This book is dedicated to my grandmother Otila Coronado, whose personal sacrifice and dedication to the education of her children has had such a profound influence on so many lives. Also, to my parents, Maria Guadalupe and Arnoldo Cuellar, who along with their love and support managed to instill in me their values, and perhaps their greatest gift of all, the opportunity of an education. Finally, this book is also dedicated to the memory of my dear friend Ron Newman, who died in 2010. Without Ron's steadfast encouragement and inspiration, these stories would never have been penned.

Special thanks to some special friends, Atilano Salas and Frank Krull, who gave of their time and ample talents to mentor me through the sometimes daunting art of writing.

EDITING: DEBORAH GONZALES

Preface

Personally, I hadn't spent much time attempting to figure out exactly who this individual was that people called Arnoldo, and I simply called "me". Most of my adulthood had been spent getting started in my profession and raising a family, so, frankly, it just hadn't seemed all that important to ponder this question too deeply. Yet, routine events occurring on a seemingly ordinary day can sometimes whisk you away in an unanticipated whirlwind of self-discovery. This happened to me one fateful day, and in the aftermath I came away with an extraordinary new perspective on my life. This unexpected revelation has given me the inspiration to share some stories of the people, places, and events that have given meaning to my life and shaped the character of this person I call "me".

1

Coronado's Garage

The day began just as most Saturdays around my house did, with me perched in my usual spot at the kitchen table, leisurely reading the morning newspaper while I sipped from a tall glass of Tropicana orange juice. I was savoring every tangy swallow as I perused the front-page headlines. Seems that on this particular day, I was a little distracted from my normal Saturday morning ritual by an object just barely in view out of the corner of my eye. What was this distraction that had me so preoccupied? And why was I so uneasy? I mused.

I could see that old, red utility trailer parked in my driveway, sitting there, just waiting to be hitched to my car. I did my best to ignore it, but it was to no avail. I knew that sooner or later I'd have to tackle that unpleasant duty that I had so far unsuccessfully tried to block out of my mind.

My interest in the editorial page quickly fizzled as the day's plans were already stewing in my mind, and I had a gut feeling that I had better be getting an early start, since this project I was planning would likely consume most of my day. So, I put down the newspaper, gathered up my leather work gloves and headed straight for the driveway, where I began the arduous task of lifting the neck of the heavy trailer and hitching it to my car.

A soft amber glow in the eastern sky greeted me as I stepped outside, and my eyes were drawn immediately towards the horizon as I watched the sun rise on a magnificent March morning. Wiping the dripping beads of sweat from my forehead, I continued my work, pausing only briefly to admire the first few rays of sunlight glimmering on the calm waters of the Corpus Christi Bay. There's a revitalizing, almost palpable sense of renewal that a South Texas spring morning sunrise exudes. There were things to do, but today I needed just another minute to soak in a little inspiration from this seasonal harbinger of renewed hope.

Now reinvigorated, with a new sense of resolve and forgetting the salty wetness that drenched my forehead, I continued my adventure of attempting to position the hitch over the two-inch ball on the rear bumper of my Toyota. After a brief but grueling round of wrestling with the obstinate utility trailer, I was finally able to position the hitch over the illusive chrome ball, and it dropped into place with a reassuring "thud". I smiled smugly and placed my foot on the trailer hitch, imagining I was Clint Eastwood in a *Dirty Harry* movie, placing his foot on the neck of a captured criminal while defiantly uttering, "Make my day."

Now, all that remained was to secure the lock and fasten the safety chains. Wiping the grimy black globs of grease from my gloves, I called out to my wife, "Jan, I'm ready." The two of us climbed into the car, and we headed out on our dutiful journey. Eighty miles west lay our destination, Benavides, the small South Texas town where I had grown up. These frequent trips to Benavides had always been pleasant journeys in the past, but the sequence of events that had led up to this particular trip had put a damper on my normal feelings of anticipation.

Just recently, after my mother's eighty-eighth birthday, we had helped her relocate into an assisted living facility in Corpus Christi, Texas, where she could be closer to us. Until now, her life had been firmly rooted in Benavides, the place where she had grown up, met my father and raised a family of her own. It hadn't been an easy decision for her to leave her home of so many years; however, she knew deep down that it was the right decision.

My father Arnoldo, whom I was named after, had passed away in 1985, leaving her to run the household alone for the last twenty-four years. Guadalupe, my mother, had managed it well until her health began to decline, and she was no longer able to live independently. Jan and I were headed back to collect the last remaining household possessions from the life she had known for so very long.

It seems that we had found a buyer for our old house, and it needed to be readied for occupancy. Mother had struggled with the idea of selling the home that she and my father had created from their shared life and love; however, a recently divorced mother of two named Yvette had shown a genuine fondness for the house and proved to be very persistent in her desire to buy it. Eventually, my mother succumbed and consented to the sale. She took great comfort in knowing that Yvette and her children might once again bring life and love into this very special abode. Mother would sever her last ties to Benavides and begin her new life in Corpus Christi.

The small community of Benavides, where I was raised, had been an oil boomtown in the 1940s, and in its heyday boasted a population of over three thousand, with over eighty businesses. Thriving oil companies had moved entire families into the town and in the process, brought prosperity with them. The economy was robust and the little municipality flourished. The schools were first rate and regularly produced graduates who ventured to pursue careers as teachers, physicians, engineers, lawyers and successful businessmen. Many of them returned to live and work in the confines of this South Texas community, where they had been raised and nurtured. My mother and her three sisters had graduated from Benavides schools, and all but her sister Macarita had returned to teach in the highly regarded Benavides school system.

Benavides had always been a tight knit community where citizens expressed their civic-minded pride, and neighbors looked out for one another. Many a business deal was sealed with a promise and a handshake. A man's word was his bond, and the locals didn't see much need for signed contracts and lawyers. Benavides was a friendly place and, like the title song from the television series *Cheers* says, "a place where everybody knows your name." This was a good thing in the reality of an adult world, but for us kids who sometimes failed to grasp adult things, it was somewhat like living in a fish bowl, our every movement visible for all to see. Well-intentioned townspeople were in ample supply, and always more than willing to notify our parents if word got around that we might be involved in any questionable activities, whatever "questionable" might mean. Though many of us felt that our personal growth was somewhat stifled by this constant communal supervision, it was probably a good thing because it kept a lot of us from getting into any serious trouble in our formative years. All in all, Benavides's citizenry was its life's blood, and all of these people made it a great place to live and raise a family.

Unfortunately, the oil reserves in the outlying oilfields had been relatively small and shallow, and by the 1970s, the steady stream of oil that had allowed Benavides to thrive had been reduced to a mere trickle. Since the local economy had been built primarily on oil revenue, as the oil reserves dwindled, so did prosperity in the little boomtown. By the 1970s, the same fine school system that had produced more than its share of successful graduates could no longer provide employment opportunities for local graduates who wanted to return. One by one, the young began an inevitable and steady exodus. Businesses closed their doors by the dozens, families moved and Benavides fell on hard times.

Jan and I continued our trek westward on that old, familiar route, Highway 359, to the place where I had grown up. I had made this hour and a half drive so many times in the past that I could practically navigate it in my sleep; however, there was something weighing heavily on my mind this time around. Was it guilt? I remembered having been the one to convince my mother to move from her residence of nearly sixty years, and I knew that it had been a painful decision for her. And while this was all true, and I certainly felt responsible for displacing her, it still wasn't what was troubling me at the moment. Then it hit me like a ton of bricks: it was an unsettling feeling that I was about to lose something immensely important to me. I had come to the painful realization that I was about to sever my last physical connection to Benavides, that small South Texas community that had played such a vital role in my life.

As we approached that oh-so-recognizable hill that offered a panoramic view of the city, I was overcome by feelings that I had experienced before, but in a very different sense. It was as if a thick fog had lifted, revealing to me that my hometown, a place that I had always expected to be there, patiently waiting to welcome me with open arms like a faithful old friend, had all but disappeared. Was this simply a sense of loss? I wondered. I had experienced those feelings before when my father had passed away, but this feeling was distinctly different. It involved the loss of my youthful innocence that was embodied by my hometown.

Sure, most of the old buildings were still there and still fostered fond memories; nonetheless, I was beginning to realize that my real connection to Benavides had been through the love and vitality of the relationships I had forged with my friends and family. Sadly, most of these people were no longer around. A lot of my friends had relocated to other communities in search of employment, and many of my relatives had either moved or passed away. I knew that my mother had been the last remaining bond I had with Benavides, and now that she was leaving, I was left with an unfamiliar sense of emptiness and sadness in my life.

The Benavides I knew had served as a reassuring and steadfast beacon in the uncharted oceans of my life. It had always been a reference point from which I had measured all my successes and my failures. The town had helped me define who I was today and where my life's sojourn had led me. I was beginning to feel a definite void in my life, as if I had lost a lifelong friend and companion.

This was the moment in time when it all started to become exceedingly clear to me, and by "it", I mean my life. What followed was an epiphany of sorts, and a new understanding of the evolution of this person people call Arnoldo.

I must have been totally immersed in these thoughts because the next thing I knew, I was driving past the Kwik Pantry convenience store that now occupied the hallowed ground where my grandfather's Gulf service station once proudly stood. "Coronado's Garage" is a place that now exists only in my mind, but nevertheless it remains a wondrous place that harbored a thousand precious memories of my youth.

I found myself absorbed in vivid memories of Coronado's Garage, consumed by recollections of those marvelous days of youthful innocence and images of the people and places that helped shaped my life.

Coronado's Garage, circa 1940

2

A Working Man

"Wake up, wake up! It's time to rise and shine!" My mother's rousing wake-up call reverberated through my bedroom door on that June summer morning. I was ten years old, and there was something very special about this particular summer morning. I had set my alarm clock for 6 a.m. to make sure I was up at the crack of dawn because I didn't want to miss a single minute of this day of days. I shot out of bed like a lightning bolt, hurriedly brushed my teeth, ran a comb through my hair, put on a pair of denim jeans, and then fished out my best white t-shirt from the dresser drawer. I was almost ready but just needed one more thing. I hurried out to my father's workshop to find that oil-stained red rag that was to be part of my uniform. With a grease monkey's trademark identity tucked in my back pocket, I was now ready to report to Coronado's Garage for my first day on the job. Yes, sir, I was now a working man.

Until that morning, it had been a pretty uneventful summer, so I had complained to my parents that I was bored. They seemed genuinely concerned and offered to help me with a solution to my dilemma. Their recommendation was that I look for summer employment, and they suggested that I speak to Pedro Coronado, the proprietor of Coronado's Garage, to set up an interview for a job at the gas station. I wasted no time and asked them to drive me there. Upon arrival I went through what at the time seemed to be a grueling interview process, in which I promptly stated my credentials for the position. "Assistant attendant in charge of insect removal from automobile windshields" was a position of great responsibility, but I felt that I was well qualified for the job. I had practiced cleaning the bugs off of my father's 1959 Nash Metropolitan many times, so I was very proficient with a sponge and a chamois cloth. All I needed was an opportunity to display my talents.

1959 Nash Metropolitan

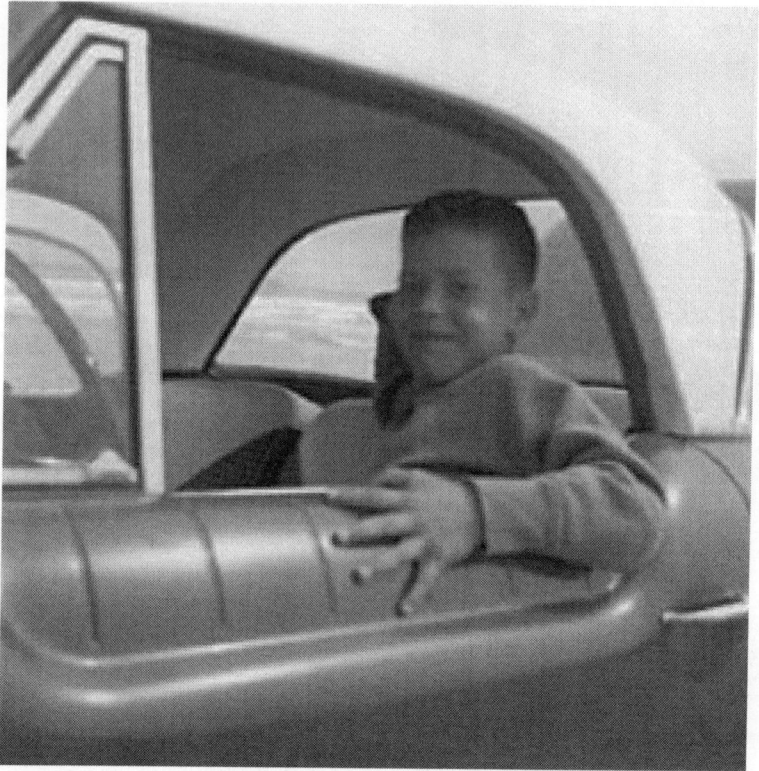

Arnoldo X. Cuellar, age 8

Pedro Coronado was obviously a very good judge of character because he hired me right on the spot. I would be making a very lucrative salary of four dollars per week. Not bad for a ten year old. It never occurred to me that Pedro's hiring decision may have been influenced by the fact that I was his grandson, since I was obviously well qualified for the job and would no doubt be an asset to the whole operation.

The morning rush hour began at about 7 a.m., when the working crowd pulled in to gas up on their way to school or work. This year had been a banner year for butterflies and bugs, so it seemed that every windshield had a hefty, resin-like layer of crusty insect body parts and splattered bug juice that needed to be removed. Apparently these bugs were a little more tenacious than the ones I had removed from the windshield on my dad's Metropolitan, but with the use of a step stool and a little elbow grease, I was able to get the windshields so clean that the glass practically disappeared. After about an hour of steady business the pace slowed down, and my grumbling stomach would tell me it was time for a morning snack. There went ten cents on the vending machine for a Coke and a nickel for a package of Tom's vanilla cream cookies.

Once the morning rush was over, the day seemed to drag on endlessly. There might be twenty minutes or more between customers, so I would strike up a conversation with Roberto, the number one attendant. He was a tough looking older kid who had dropped out of high school and gone to work at the station, so as you might imagine, he didn't have a lot of time for chatty ten-year-old kids. It was a short-lived conversation. I did, however, manage to extract a few useful tips from him about operating the gas pump and locating the dipstick under the hood of a car. This advice would be of great help to me in the future when I got my big chance to pump gas and check the oil level on my own. I had my eye on his job, and I knew that with a little time and experience I could convince my grandfather to let me expand my duties beyond windshield cleaning.

Upon noon's arrival, I was off to my grandmother's house for lunch. Otila Coronado lived about a block from Coronado's Garage, so it was a short hike. My grandmother was a great cook and there was always a delicious meal waiting for me. Rice and beans were the usual fare, sometimes "calabaza con pollo" (squash with chicken), and always homemade tortillas. After lunch, she and I would sit and watch her favorite soap opera, *As the World Turns*. Ma Tila, as she was affectionately known, was a truly amazing person. For a woman who spoke only a few words of English, she understood every sordid detail of the soap opera characters' lives. "Ese hombre es un sin berguenza" ("That man has no shame"), she would say about one of the actors who played the role of an unsavory character. Ma Tila might be able to overlook a multitude of character flaws, but having no shame was one that she felt was totally unforgivable. She explained the entire plot to me in Spanish and made sure I knew her take on each character in the drama. Once *As the World Turns* was over, it was time for me to head back to Coronado's Garage.

Business in the early afternoon was usually light, and the pace was slow, so I would hang around Roberto and hand him tools while he fixed flat tires. I had watched the process many times, and I was pretty sure I could help him, but he never asked, so I would stand there feeling rather useless while watching him work. Though I would sometimes get the distinct impression that he thought I was in his way, I would dismiss the perception that he was ignoring me as sign that he was just in a hurry to finish the job.

By about 2:30 p.m., it was time for an afternoon snack. Amidst the sweltering, South Texas heat, nothing would provide relief quite like a cold Coca Cola and a bag of peanuts. It was a marvelous concoction. First, I would buy an ice-cold bottle of Coke. After taking a small swig to make room for the salted peanuts, I would add the whole bag into the bottle of Coke. Finally, with a gentle swirl of the bottle to provide the proper mixing effect, this delicious concoction was ready for drinking. Peanuts would pour out with every sip of Coke, giving it a sweet and salty taste at the same time. Nothing could beat this for an afternoon refresher.

This cost me another ten cents for the Coke and a nickel for a bag of Tom's peanuts, bringing my total expenditures for snacks to thirty cents for the day. Having been one of Sister Mary Monica's prized math pupils at St. Rose of Lima Parochial School, I calculated that I was consuming 38 percent of my salary on snacks. All those difficult math problems I hated about trains moving in opposite directions had finally paid off. Oh, well. A working man needed his nourishment, and I was pretty sure that if I kept up the hard work, a raise might be in my future.

There was a cast of characters that usually made an appearance at the garage once or twice a week. They came in ostensibly to gas up, but more often than not they would step into the station, pull up a chair and chat with my grandfather. They would usually stay a while and catch up with the latest town news and gossip. My grandfather Pedro loved to exchange stories and spin tall tales with these old codgers, and Coronado's Garage had become a regular watering hole for these colorful types.

Carl Rexroad was one of these memorable locals who frequented Coronado's Garage. Mr. Rexroad was a crusty old guy who drove an old, red International Scout pick-up truck. He usually came through once or twice a week, though he didn't always purchase gas. Sometimes he just wanted to have the oil level checked, water added to his radiator or his tire pressure measured.

1960 International Scout pick up

One sunny afternoon, Mr. Rexroad drove up in his red truck and asked me to check his oil. As was his habit, he walked inside and chatted with my grandfather while I proceeded to try to open the hood to his truck. I stuck my nose in every nook and cranny of that truck trying to find the latch release lever so that I could check his oil. It was to no avail. I could not find a trace of that lever. Now, I had a real dilemma on my hands. I had wanted to impress my grandfather with my knowledge of automobiles so that he would expand my duties beyond just scraping bugs off of windshields, so I couldn't very well admit that I wasn't able to open the hood to the truck. Eventually, when Mr. Rexroad walked out and asked me how the oil level was, without hesitation, I answered, "Just fine."

I learned many valuable lessons that summer at Coronado's Garage, and that afternoon I had the privilege of learning my first. This one came to me right where I stood at the moment, courtesy of Mr. Rexroad himself. He looked me straight in the eyes and said, "Son, I watched you the entire time, and you know you never opened that hood, did you?"

If ever there was a time when a kid would like to have disappeared into thin air, this was surely it. I knew I had been caught, and there was no way out, so with all the courage I could muster, I did the only thing I could think of. Desperate times called for desperate measures, so I resorted to the unthinkable: the truth. I swallowed hard, looked at him and said, "No, sir, I didn't."

There was an awkward moment of silence that seemed to drag on forever, but then he looked at me, smiled and said, "Son, I want you to always remember that it's a hell of a lot easier to tell the truth than it is to make up a big lie." He patted me on the shoulder and proceeded to show me how to open the hood of his truck. This little piece of advice was not wasted on me, as I would recall it often for the rest of my life.

This had been a summer of discovery for a working man at Coronado's Garage. My experiences that summer taught me many lessons, including the value of money and the importance of always telling the truth when faced with difficult situations. (Or, at the very least, to look both ways to make sure no one is watching when you fib about something you did!)

Finally, the greatest and most unexpected discovery I made at the end of that glorious summer was that my parents were paying my grandfather $4 a week to employ me.

Oh, and by the way, there is one last addition to lessons learned that summer: beware of adults bearing solutions to your problems. They sometimes have ulterior motives.

℥

"Why didn't you turn left to go to your mother's house?" The inevitable question came from my wife, as I continued my drive through downtown Main Street. I suspect she knew the answer, but she felt obliged to ask anyway.

"I just wanted to drive through the old town one last time," I answered. Main Street ran parallel to the old Texas-Mexican (now Kansas City Southern) railroad tracks that split the town and the business district down the center. This one last nostalgic trek through the town would be my way of bidding a fond farewell to the place that had provided me with so many priceless memories.

These days, about the only sign of life in Benavides was the sight of an occasional passing freight train. The Kansas City Southern came thundering through the quiet little community four or five times a day, wakening the little South Texas town from its peaceful, sleep-like tranquility, with loud trumpeting blasts from its horn. The struggling local economy had been plummeting for many years, with only a handful of retail establishments managing to survive. My eyes were immediately drawn to the sight of the town's many old, dilapidated commercial buildings, decaying relics of better times. Like ancient Mayan temples lying in ruins, these crumbling monuments now dotted the gaunt landscape of the old town. I must admit that initially, I felt a little bit like Thomas Wolfe must have when he wrote, "You Can't Go Home Again," but these feelings soon gave way to more nostalgic recollections of the "pueblito" (village) and its colorful cast of characters as I remembered them from my past.

3

Let's Take A Spin

**Remnants of the old Farias General store
in downtown Benavides**

Remnants of the Piggly Wiggly grocery store

Off in the distance stood the weathered remains of the old Piggly Wiggly grocery store that had been a regular stop for me as a kid. Though the doors were securely boarded up, with a little imagination I could envision Willie Vaello, the owner, Dan Redner, the butcher, and Bertha Vaello, the checker, standing there behind the counter, waiting to greet me as they had done so many years ago. No one was a stranger at the Piggly, as we used to call it. The Vaello family had owned it since the 1930s. If you entered the store to buy groceries, you were likely to spend more time catching up on local news and town gossip than you would spend shopping. The store was family owned and operated, so townspeople had come to expect hospitality and personal attention, which had been the store's trademark for so many years.

Piggly Wiggly, circa 1940

As a kid, I had a somewhat ravenous appetite for ham sandwiches, so when I had depleted our refrigerator's stockpile of ham, my parents would drive me to the Piggly Wiggly. I would walk back to the butcher shop at the rear of the store where Dan, the butcher, would greet me and take my order. Our conversation could have just as well been scripted because it usually went like this:

"What can I do you for, young man?" he would say with a grin. "I need half a pound of boiled ham," I'd reply. With a somewhat quizzical look on his face, Dan would say, "Okay, half a pound of spoiled ham coming right up." It had become like an old Vaudeville comedy routine, and we'd both laugh every time just as if we had never spoken those lines before.

I can remember racing down the cereal aisle, the wooden floors creaking beneath my feet as I shook every box of Tony the Tiger's Frosted Flakes, trying to figure out which one might contain that most treasured prize. Perhaps one might contain a green plastic soldier, a magnifying glass, maybe even a decoder ring, or a plastic racecar with wheels that never quite seemed to stay on securely. One could only imagine all the possibilities.

There were few smells as pleasing to the senses as the sweet piney fragrance of freshly cut Christmas trees that permeated the store in early December. That was the time of year when my dad and I set out on our annual quest to find that perfectly shaped Christmas tree. Willie, the owner, would escort my dad and me into the storage room behind the meat market where he would allow us to rummage through all the trees he had in stock until we found that perfect one. Once we had selected this special tree, my dad would haul it out to the checkout counter where Bertha or Petra would ring up the sale. Most of the retail stores offered credit, so it was always a huge thrill when my dad would let me sign the charge receipt.

Just down the street were a couple of establishments that harbored even more indelible memories from my younger days. For a minute, it felt as if I had been transported back in time, and the town I used to know had come back to life. I remembered that distinctive smell of new denim jeans stacked high on the display shelves at El Nuevo Mundo, the building next door to the Piggly Wiggly.

El Nuevo Mundo was the dry goods store where my mother had purchased many of my school clothes, including the red and white St. Rose of Lima Parochial School uniforms that we were required to wear when I was in grade school. Just next door sat the empty lot that the Rita Theater used to occupy. It brought back vivid recollections of the aroma of fresh popcorn, the taste of Baby Ruth candy bars, and the flavor of Bazooka bubble gum that I used to purchase at the concession stand of the old theater, so many years ago.

El Nuevo Mundo Dry Goods Store, circa 1950

Little could compare to the excitement of getting a quarter ("peseta") and a fifty-cent piece ("toston") from my dad for a Saturday afternoon matinee at the Rita Theater. It didn't much matter to us what the feature was. It could have been a John Wayne western like *Rio Bravo* or a Jerry Lewis comedy like *The Nutty Professor*. We all loved the Saturday afternoon movies. My friends and I would laugh and tease the whole time as we wound our way through the neighborhoods on our way down the three-quarter-mile trail to the theater. Like frolicking bear cubs, we would playfully push and shove each other, as we tried to impress our buddies with our astonishing tales.

"My uncle has a new car that will go a hundred miles an hour," one kid would say.

"That's nothing, my brother has a hot rod that almost broke the sound barrier."

"I know your brother. He's barely old enough to drive, you liar, liar pants on fire."

"It's true. I promise, cross my heart and hope to die, stick a needle in my eye."

This type of banter would go back and forth until we finally lined up at the ticket booth.

The RITA
An afternoon at the movies in Benavides circa 1960

34

The seventy five cents my dad had given me would be enough to pay for the movie, a candy bar, popcorn and a Coke, with enough left over to buy a "trompo" (wooden top) on the way home at the store we called the Bus Stop. Buying a top was tricky business in those days. "Should I buy the red one? No, the green one might spin better. What the heck, I'll get the blue one." Tops were valuable commodities back then because they were used in a competition that allowed a young boy to prove his skill and gain acceptance amongst his peers.

The game went like this: First, a mark was drawn on the ground. Each contestant would wind a "cuerda" (string) around their top and sling it at the target. The boy whose top spun furthest from the mark would have to place his top on the ground, becoming the new target. The others would then spin again, aiming carefully at the target, trying to inflict damage on it with the points of their own tops. A direct hit was called a "canco". If a player was unable to hit the top with his spin, he would be required to place his top on the ground for the other kids to use as their target. The older boys spent hours sharpening the points on their tops for this purpose. If anyone managed to impale the point of his top on the target top, it became his property. As it is said, "To the victor belong the spoils."

As you might imagine, the older boys walked away with many of my new tops, and I can still remember the sick feeling in the pit of my stomach when one of the older kids, took ownership of my favorite top. Oh well. Hope sprang eternally in the Benavides of my youth. There would always be next week, when my dad would give me more movie money so that I could catch the latest western at the Rita and buy another new top at the Bus Stop on the way home.

&

My wife and I continued on our leisurely drive through town. On the left were the remnants of Nap Chandler's Texaco Station. Nap's station and Coronado's Garage, in their time, were the premier full service gas stations in town. Though they were fierce competitors in business, Pedro and Nap were well-respected, ethical businessmen who coexisted in the little town as good personal friends and fellow Rotarians.

Nap Chandler's Texas Station 1950s

Further down the road was Marin's Drive-In. It had been our version of Arnold's Drive-In from *Happy Days*. Marin's griddle served up delicious old-fashioned greasy burgers and fries. The great food, along with the satisfaction of eating with your friends in your own car, quickly made Marin's the popular local hangout for high school students after football games and dances. With one flash of your headlights, a carhop (or Marin himself) would be out to take your order. Within five or ten minutes, you'd have a metal tray hanging on your driver's side window loaded with burgers, fries, milkshakes or any one of a dozen other fast food items. A little short on money? No problem. If your parents had a solid reputation in town, Marin's offered you credit, so you could run up a tab and pay later.

4

Happy Daze

Back in my high school days, my good friend and classmate, Atilano Salas, had run up a thirty-five dollar tab at Marin's Drive-In, unbeknownst to his parents. This may not sound like much today, but it was a sizeable sum back in the sixties. He had fully intended to settle his account, but his appetite for fast food had far exceeded his meager ability to pay. One Saturday night, as Atilano drove his father's old pick-up truck and parked under that old, familiar corrugated tin awning, Marin walked out to meet him with charge receipts in hand. In a somewhat stern, fatherly tone, he admonished Atilano: "I can't let you charge no more, until you pay." Marin was a man of few words, but Atilano got his message loud and clear. Marin could easily have threatened to go to Atilano's father for payment, but instead he felt it was more important that Atilano have a chance to redeem himself and learn a lesson in responsibility on his own.

Marin's Drive In, 1963

Atilano was embarrassed by the situation but thankful for the chance at redemption. He found a job and worked diligently that summer to earn enough money to settle his debt. When he had earned enough to make payment in full, he made it a point to personally hand deliver the cash to Marin. He found Marin seated in his usual spot, perched on the well-worn, vinyl-upholstered chrome stool, from which he lorded over the entire fast food operation. As Atilano walked over to pay Marin, he was filled with feelings of both embarrassment for having taken so long to settle his debt and gratitude for the second chance Marin had given him. Marin took the money, shook his hand, smiled and said, "I have something for you." He thanked Atilano for honoring his commitment and handed him a six-pack of soft drinks in appreciation. Atilano politely declined Marin's generous gift out of sheer embarrassment, but

Marin would not take no for an answer, so Atilano graciously accepted Marin's token of appreciation. Marin beamed with pride as he walked slowly back to his stool, satisfied that his mission had been accomplished.

It was obvious that getting payment had been of secondary importance to Marin. Foremost in his mind was the idea of helping Atilano become a more responsible citizen in the community. Stories like this were commonplace in Benavides. The tradition of townspeople helping parents raise good solid citizens had become the hallmark of this little South Texas community for many years.

Marin's Drive-In was a place where great memories were made and many life lessons were learned. It had been a haven for teenagers in Benavides since the 1950s, and if you ever ask anyone who grew up in Benavides about Marin's, they would probably have an amusing story or two to tell you. It was an institution in our little town, and its closing in the 1980s marked the end of a very special era in the history of Benavides.

At the far west end of town, bordered by the mesquite laden brush country, was my old high school. Cruising by the campus brought back vivid memories of those marvelous feelings of the first day of class each school year. I remembered the unmistakable smell of freshly sharpened pencils and new textbooks, and how we carefully folded those tan book covers with the Benavides Eagle mascot in the center, bordered by ads for the local businesses. We neatly folded each crease on those covers as if our efforts foretold the grade we would receive in that particular course.

We also drove by the old ball field where Billy Ray Nelson from West Oso High had hit my first pitch on opening day of my senior year over the center field fence. Though I probably didn't find the humor in it back then, I couldn't help but chuckle about it now.

This was the same high school where my Aunt Gloria had been the librarian, and my mother served as the sophomore and senior English teacher. If there had been an upside to this scenario, other than always having a ride to school, I certainly could not have told you what it was. With all of these watchful eyes hovering over me, I felt as if I had been under constant surveillance, and I was always envious of my friends whose relatives had no connection to the school.

My mother had been an excellent teacher, but she was a real stickler for discipline in her classroom. Bad behavior was not tolerated in her class, and any student who dared challenge her authority ended up at the principal's office for disciplining. As you might imagine, this didn't go over well with the rowdier kids in school. I learned quickly that these kids would take every opportunity to make my life as miserable as possible in retaliation.

One day during my freshman year, I was changing into my gym shorts for P.E. class when one of the senior kids, Jesus "Chuey" Garza, decided that I was fair game for a baptismal ceremony at the boy's dressing room urinal. Chuey (pronounced like "chewy") had coaxed several of his friends into grabbing me by my arms and legs. The plan was to place my head in the urinal and flush it while the onlookers had a good laugh at my expense. Chuey was a bully, one of those kids who was always in trouble and wasn't afraid to use his fists to settle his disputes. Few kids challenged his authority. Earlier, my mother had sent him to the principal's office for discipline, and he had decided to take his frustration out on me. He knew that I wouldn't say a word to my mother for fear of being known around the school as a "stoolie" (tattletale). He was correct. It was bad enough being a teacher's kid. I didn't want to add the title "informant" to my already tenuous resume.

The practice of hazing freshmen had been a long-standing tradition in high school, so lowly freshmen expected to be harassed by the upper classmen. But this time, I felt that Chuey's prank had gone a little too far. I wasn't the kind of kid to get into fights, but the idea of having my head dunked in the urinal while my friends watched didn't appeal to me in the least. So, since I was a skinny kid, I managed to break away from the grip of the mob just long enough to grab a Converse All Star tennis shoe out of my gym storage basket. Chuey, now more determined than ever to dunk me in the urinal, came back after me. I tightly gripped the shoe in my right hand and with all the strength I could muster, I hit him across the chest with it.

I'm not sure who was more surprised about this sequence of events: me or Chuey. For an instant, we both stood there in disbelief at what had just transpired. Emblazoned across his hairy, pale-skinned chest was the red, waffle-like imprint of the sole of my size 9 ½ Converse All Star tennis shoe. I thought to myself, "Did I just do what I think I did?"

I wasn't too sure if I should be scared or proud of my accomplishment. As it turned out, I didn't have much time to stand there and admire my handiwork because the next thing I felt was the burning sting of Chuey's fist on the side of my head. I dropped to the floor and staggered to my feet like Stallone in a final-round scene of *Rocky*. By this time, the ruckus had attracted the attention of Coach Rivera, our P.E. instructor. Fortunately for me, he came in and separated the two of us before Chuey had the opportunity to get any more punches in. We were both taken into his office and received what we called "licks" (blows to our butts with a paddle). This was the standard punishment for fighting. Even though Chuey probably got the best of this confrontation, I couldn't help but beam with pride when the news of the fight spread through the hallways at school. Not many kids would stand up to Chuey, but I had. Or, at least I acted as if I would have if coach Rivera hadn't separated us. I wore my puffy eye as a red badge of courage the rest of that day. A far as my mother ever knew, it was a basketball injury.

I'm not sure if Chuey ever graduated from high school, but several years later I heard a rumor that he had stabbed a man to death in a fight at a local bar called the Silver Night. It made me wonder if fate had been on my side that day, because that dead guy might have been me if Coach Rivera hadn't come in and broken up the fight when he did.

გ

Jan had indulged me by letting me have one last nostalgic jaunt around the old town, but now it was time to return to the business at hand and load up the trailer with my mother's personal belongings. I took one last wistful look back at the old high school, turned the car around and headed in the direction of my mother's house. We drove east toward La Mota Street, which was a narrow stretch of asphalt that coursed eastward by mother's house and eventually connected with Highway 2295 toward Kingsville. It was a dangerous road that had definitely been off limits to me and my bike as a kid.

5

King of the Hill

"Don't ride your bicycle on the highway." These words of caution resonated in my head, but like the sound of birds chirping on a spring morning, they were only background noise. They hadn't soaked in because, at least in my mind, they were just "momspeak", obligatory words of caution that all mothers had been genetically programmed to spew out to their children. They had not registered in my brain, and for all intents and purposes, my mother might as well have been speaking Chinese.

I had ridden the same old Pee Wee Herman-style bicycle with the big fat tires and the big fenders for five years. It was the same bicycle that my dad had placed training wheels on when I first got it. But one Christmas morning, I had found a brand new red, three-speed Schwinn bike under my Christmas tree. This baby was built for speed, and I was just chomping at the bit to put it through its paces.

My friend, Simon Saenz, and I had talked about taking a bicycle excursion to La Mota Creek, which was about four miles east of town on the highway toward Kingsville. La Mota Creek (commonly referred to as "La Mota") was an intriguing but somewhat mysterious place; an old, dry creek bed bordered by large Hackberry and Mesquite trees. It was the place where many of the town's people had their big Easter celebrations. La Mota was the perfect location for a family picnic because of its picturesque back country setting with an abundance of shade trees. Shade was a premium commodity in the brush country around Benavides. Because of the creek's remoteness, miles from civilization, it was also a great place for young boys to explore nature, look for arrowheads and dig up old artifacts. Looking back on it, I'm sure the allure of this remote wilderness destination was largely due to the wondrous faux feeling of independence and self-reliance we had when we were off the radar screen of parental supervision. As it turned out, this powerful attraction proved to be too much for my curiosity to resist.

La Mota Creek had become shrouded in local folklore as an intriguing place where unexplained apparitions frequently occurred. There was a legend that people driving on the highway by this dry creek at night had been chased by a mysterious ball of fire that followed their automobiles for miles before it would suddenly disappear. Even in my college years I can remember looking over my shoulder more than once and turning up the volume on the radio as I drove past this spooky creek at night on my way home from Kingsville.

My friend Simon was the youngest of nine children. His parents had probably given up any hopes of keeping track of all their children, so he had a lot more personal freedom than I did. Being an only child, I always envied the freedom he had to go where he pleased without having to ask permission, while I, on the other hand, had to contend with what I perceived to be a restrictive tyrannical regime at home. I knew that it was going to be next to impossible for me to get my parent's permission to go to La Mota on my bicycle, so I decided to adhere to the old adage that says, "It is easier to ask for forgiveness than it is to ask for permission." Off we went to La Mota on our big adventure.

It was not at all unusual for me to tell my parents that I was going to a neighbor's house to throw around the baseball for a couple of hours, so this story would provide us the cover and the time to head out on the open highway to La Mota Creek on our bicycles. Simon and I headed out on the open road, feeling as free as the South Texas wind blowing at our backs. Our first rendezvous with adventure that afternoon was at "La Loma" (The Hill), as the locals knew it. By South Texas standards, this was a formidable hill. It was about a mile east of town on the road to La Mota Creek. This hill was already well into restricted space, definitely a no-ride-zone as far as my parents were concerned.

At the top of this hill sat an abandoned stone shack that had been built in the 1800s. The roof had partially collapsed, but much of the interior was still intact. The building was also part of the local folklore. Legend had it that this place had been a hideout for some notorious outlaws before the turn of the century. I had watched enough television Westerns to believe that this explanation was entirely plausible. As we walked through the rubble, I could almost hear the sound of a tinny piano with the bad guys drinking, cussing and playing poker in the background. It looked like the perfect place to search for buried treasure, or at least some old coins or arrowheads half-buried in the dirt. We scoured the area but could turn up only a few pointy rocks that we convinced ourselves were old arrowheads. We only had a two-hour window of opportunity, so there was no time to waste. We mounted our bikes and continued east three more miles down the highway to La Mota Creek.

Finally, we arrived at our destination. We hid our bikes in the tall weeds so that cars passing by couldn't see that we were there. Simon and I set out on foot to explore the old, dry creek bed that was lined on both sides by large trees. The further away we got from the highway, the denser the foliage became. Darkening shadows gradually took on an ominous quality, as an eerie quiet enveloped us while we continued to explore. Down a ways, we found an old rope that someone had tied to a large tree to swing from one side of the creek bed to the other. We climbed the tree and proceeded to try to swing and let out a yell just as Tarzan did in the movies. We had wandered about half a mile from the highway, and I could swear that I heard the sound of faint voices off in the distance. The eerie surroundings had gotten a little too creepy for my taste by now, so I was more than ready to head back to the highway. I convinced Simon that we needed to head back home before my parents figured out that I wasn't pitching baseballs at a neighbor's house.

But we had one final stop to make. About half way back home was the local wastewater treatment plant. This place was definitely off limits to us, but it was the only place in town where we could find cattails. These cattails, which we called "punks", were an extremely valuable commodity for young boys our age. Once dried out, they could be lit with a match and would burn for hours. They were an excellent source of fire with which to light "cohetes" (fireworks).

There was no shortage of fireworks in Benavides. As young boys we spent much of our free time igniting them, especially around the holidays. We had planned to gather a stockpile of these cattails, enough to last us the entire year. The problem was that the cattails only grew at the water's edge where the mud was extremely soft, like quicksand. The thought of sinking up to our necks in quicksand, like we had seen in the movies, just added an element of danger to the mission, which made the adventure even more exciting. We finally managed to harvest about a dozen of these cattails without casualties by me holding Simon's hand as he stretched his arms over the swampy water to grab the elusive prize. We cleaned the mud off our shoes, stuffed the cattails in our pockets and headed back home, like conquering heroes.

We had accomplished our objectives, and it was time to head for home. However, one last great challenge lay before us. It was "La Loma", that seemingly monolithic rise in the otherwise flat brush county that had never been conquered on a bicycle. I could almost hear it snickering at us, daring us to take it on. It was to be the ultimate challenge. Simon and I had talked about taking it on several times, but now the time had come for us to humble the treacherous "La Loma", full speed, no holds barred, downhill on our bikes. We coasted to a stop at the top of the hill and surveyed the steep grade, making sure that there were no cars coming in either direction on the highway. We had each brought a clothespin and a baseball trading card. The card was clipped on the frame of our bikes so that the spokes clattering against the cards made a motorized sound. The loud, staccato, engine-like sound was guaranteed to give us the full effect of the speeds we were about to achieve. I'm sure that many priceless Mickey Mantle rookie trading cards bit the dust in this manner.

On the count of three, with our hearts pounding and adrenalin pumping, we started pedaling with full force down the foreboding hill—Simon, on his tank of a bike with the big tires, and me on my new sleek Schwinn three-speed racer. About a third of the way down I began feeling a slight vibration on the handlebars. The next thing I knew the world was spinning around me and I was flying through the air in what seemed to be slow motion. During this fraction of a second that I was floating through the air, I could hear my mother's words echoing in my head: "Don't ride your bicycle on the highway." The next thing I felt was a jolting thud, as though a sack of potatoes had smashed onto the asphalt. I was reminded of the old classic Wiley Coyote cartoon, where he takes one last step off the edge of the cliff and ends up as a puff of dust after a long fall to the bottom; only this time, I was Wiley Coyote.

When I finally opened my eyes and shook off the stars circling around my head, all I could see was Simon standing over me with a look of horror on his face. That look on his face and the sight of my front tire rim bent like a taco shell told me that I was going to have a lot of explaining to do when, and if ever, I got home. Simon helped wipe the blood off my face and removed the asphalt rocks from the strawberry-like scrapes I had on my face, arms and legs. He helped me to my feet, and we began that long painful journey, limping home with the mangled remains of my new bicycle in tow. This pitiful procession was certainly not the triumphant return we had envisioned when we started out on our mission. We had expected to return home as the conquering heroes, but somehow we had fallen short, and we returned bloodied and battered, looking more like the conquered.

I feel like I understand what an inmate must feel when he makes that long, lonely march to the gas chamber. My parents rarely used corporal punishment, so I knew I was probably safe on that count. Besides, how much fun could it be to beat on a kid that already looked as if he had been in a train wreck? I fully expected to be spending a lot of time in my room without any roaming privileges, subjected to countless lectures about showing more responsibility.

Fortunately, and to my surprise, when I got home my parents were more concerned about my injuries than they were about punishing me for my irresponsible behavior. Parents: just when you think you've figured them out, they go and do something like this. My dad wasted no time repairing my bike, and within a few days, I was riding again—a little bruised and battered, but possibly a little wiser. Now that I have children of my own I can finally appreciate how my parents handled all the difficult situations I placed them in.

ဢ

Now, with our trailer in tow, Jan and I turned right off of La Mota Street, past my friend Simon's old house, and headed down Second Street to my mother's house. Simon's house was vacant and hardly resembled the place where Don Simon and Doña Eliza, Simon's parents, had raised their nine children. ("Don" and "Doña" are formal terms of respect in the Spanish culture used by younger people when addressing an older person, a slightly more formal term than "señor" and "señora".) On the left, next door to my mother's house was the vacant lot where we used to play sandlot baseball on Saturday mornings.

6

Let's Play Ball

"I get first pick. I'll take Beto."

"If you choose Beto, then I'll take Eddie."

"Okay if you pick Eddie, then you have to take his brother, Archie."

"That's not fair. Archie is only nine."

"Well, then you can take his little brother J.P., too. They can play in right field together."

"Beto can hit home runs. How come you get him, and we get Archie and J.P.? That's not fair."

"Well, next time you get to pick first, you can pick Beto."

"Okay, but you're a cheater, cheater pumpkin eater."

These types of negotiations could be heard almost every Saturday morning emanating from the vacant lot next to my house. My parents owned this piece of property, and on Saturday mornings, come rain or shine, this dusty, sometimes grass burr-infested parcel of land was transformed into a makeshift baseball diamond for the neighborhood kids. The players' ages varied anywhere from eight to about sixteen, so intense negotiations like these were necessary to maintain some semblance of parity in the teams.

The selection process began with the two best players, who were the team captains. One would flip the bat up to the other, who would then catch the middle of the barrel with one hand. They would then alternate placing hands one above the other until the last player to fit his hand on the handle without touching the knob at the end would get first pick of players. Sounds pretty straightforward, doesn't it? Actually, there were some strategy options available to the captains that complicated the process. If one captain felt that he might not be able to grasp the bat in his hand without touching the knob at the end of the handle, he could opt to use his index and third finger to grip the bat in a scissor-like fashion instead of using his entire hand. The other captain would usually employ the same strategy. Then, fingers were placed one above the other until the end of the barrel was reached, and a winner was declared.

The process rarely ended without an argument about whether the last person's finger was actually on the bat without touching the knob.

"You're pushing my finger out of the way to make room for yours."

"No, I'm not, look it fits."

"Let's do it over."

"No way, I won fair and square."

This debate usually lasted a minute or two until one kid reluctantly gave in. Sometimes the loser would be offered "first bat", as we called it, in exchange for their concession. Once these matters were settled, it was time to play ball.

The boundaries of the field, while arbitrary, were very important to the game. The right field foul line was along an imaginary line from home plate to Eva Barton's clothesline. Left field was marked by the telephone pole at the intersection of Second Street and La Mota Street. There were usually two or three kids that could hit homers, so it was important to define the home run boundaries. The left field home run boundary was La Mota Street itself. Any ball that carried in the air and landed on any part of the street was considered a home run. The left fielder had a very dangerous position because he might occasionally have to run into oncoming traffic to field a fly ball. By the grace of God, we managed to avoid any serious injuries, despite the hazardous conditions. We did occasionally have an angry motorist stop and yell at us for making them slam on their brakes as a player or ball wandered into traffic. We dismissed this as just a minor nuisance. Irate drivers never deterred us from our weekly game.

The right field home run boundary was Eva Barton's house. If a ball hit any part of the house or the out building where she did her washing, it was declared a home run. Fortunately most of the home runs were hit to left field, but occasionally one of the older boys would hit a ball that landed on top of, or against, the Barton's house. Eva would come out and give us a piece of her mind, usually threatening to call the police. We'd normally stop the game, pick up our equipment, and act as if we were going home; but as soon as she walked back inside her house, the game was on again, as if nothing had happened.

Selecting the bases was another important task. If we could find an old cardboard box, we would cut it up to make our bases; but if not, we would improvise. Sometimes the bases were made of old aluminum Coke cans or milk cartons that we pressed into service. If we were extremely desperate, piles of caliche rocks would serve as our bases. We were quite resourceful and always managed to make do with whatever materials we had. The locations of the bases might vary from game to game, depending on who was designated to set them out. They sometimes moved from inning to inning because players often kicked them around during the game. It didn't really matter to us as long as they were somewhere in plain sight.

Some days, when there were not enough kids to field two teams, the rules of the game would have to be modified. When this happened, we would play with two bases. Second base would become first base, and home plate would remain just where it had always been. We would no longer play in teams; instead, it was every man for himself. There would be a catcher, pitcher, first baseman, and everyone else would play outfield. The object was for each player to score as many runs as he could. This was considerably more difficult than usual because there was a longer distance to first base. If you managed to get to first base, the catcher would bat so that you could try to score from first base. If you scored a run, you got to bat again. If you made an out, you'd have to play outfield and wait your turn to rotate back into the batter's position. You were responsible for remembering how many runs you scored and when it was your turn to bat. The first baseman would move to the pitcher's position, and the pitcher would move to play catcher as they rotated towards the batting position. There was only one exception: anyone who managed to catch a fly ball was entitled to go straight to the batter's box. As you might expect, the older kids managed to catch most of the fly balls, and the younger kids like me played in the outfield most of the time and didn't get to bat very often. It didn't matter all that much to me because I was thrilled just to be playing with the big guys in the first place.

These sandlot games usually started at about 10 a.m. after we had a chance to watch the Saturday morning T.V. serials like *Sky King*, *The Cisco Kid* and *The Lone Ranger*. Games usually lasted two or three hours, or until we started hearing the dreaded shouts of "Come eat your lunch!" bellowing through the neighborhood like a muezzin calling Allah's faithful to prayer.

After several ignored calls for lunch, someone's mother would usually show up with hands on hips, demanding that her boy come home that instant to eat. "Don't make me have to ask your father to come get you," came the inevitable threats. When the number of players had dwindled sufficiently, we would declare an official end of the game for the day. The game would normally have been resumed later in the afternoon, but some days were reserved for our weekly trip to the movies at the Rita Theater. So, reluctantly, we would head home for lunch, taking consolation in knowing that there was a full slate of activities still on our agenda for the afternoon.

During baseball season, Saturday afternoons were spent watching major league baseball game on television. This was a chance to see our favorite baseball heroes like Mickey Mantle, Willie Mays and Roger Maris in action. There were only two television channels available to us back then, one of which included CBS network. Fortunately for us, CBS broadcasted the New York Yankees game of the week. We would watch for hours as Dizzy Dean gave his colorful analysis of the game and touted the virtues of Falstaff Beer during the commercial breaks. Dizzy had a very distinctive vernacular all of his own, and thanks to Dizzy, it wasn't until later in my school years that I discovered that "slood" was not the past tense of "slide". Pee Wee Reese, Dizzy's broadcast partner, did the play-by-play commentary. We watched the game intently as our favorite players stepped up to the plate. Mantle, Maris, Yastrzemski and Mays were all household names in those days, and our sandlot real estate provided us with the perfect venue to emulate our favorite heroes.

We hardly ever missed the opportunity to break out our baseball equipment and play our much-anticipated Saturday morning sandlot game. Sometimes we would play so often that the seams on the baseball would begin to unravel. No problem. If we didn't have a spare ball, we would get some white bandage tape and wrap the ball up tightly, like a mummy, just to keep the game going a little longer. We were quite resourceful when it came to engaging in our favorite pastime. Not rain, cold, heat, or even the foreboding calls to lunch from our mothers could have kept us from our appointed Saturday morning ritual. If baseball was indeed America's game, then we were undoubtedly great Americans.

In preparation for the major leagues of life, sandlot baseball was like spring training camp for young boys like us. It was an integral part of our youth, and while it was great fun, it taught us many valuable lessons about life and human nature. Our little sandlot prepared us for coping with situations in an adult world into which we would inevitably be thrust.

∽

Next stop was my mother's house. Jan opened that old chain link gate, and I backed the trailer into that old, familiar driveway. This time, though, there was something strangely different about the old house. The exterior of the house recently had received a complete makeover. The old asbestos siding and Permastone (faux brickwork) had been removed and given way to a modern looking HardiPlank veneer. Just as I began to think that this house was not the one I remembered from my youth, I walked inside and everything changed. The first thing that caught my eye as I stepped through the doorway was the breakfast bar that connected the kitchen to the dining room. This breakfast bar immediately brought back many fond recollections. I saw my mother serve about a thousand scrambled eggs on that counter with twice as many homemade flour tortillas. My father, with a steaming coffee mug clutched in his hand, had also been a regular fixture at this counter for as long as I could remember. Across the breakfast bar lay the dining room and the table where I had spent many evenings diligently draped over my schoolwork.

7

Coffee Cup Calculations

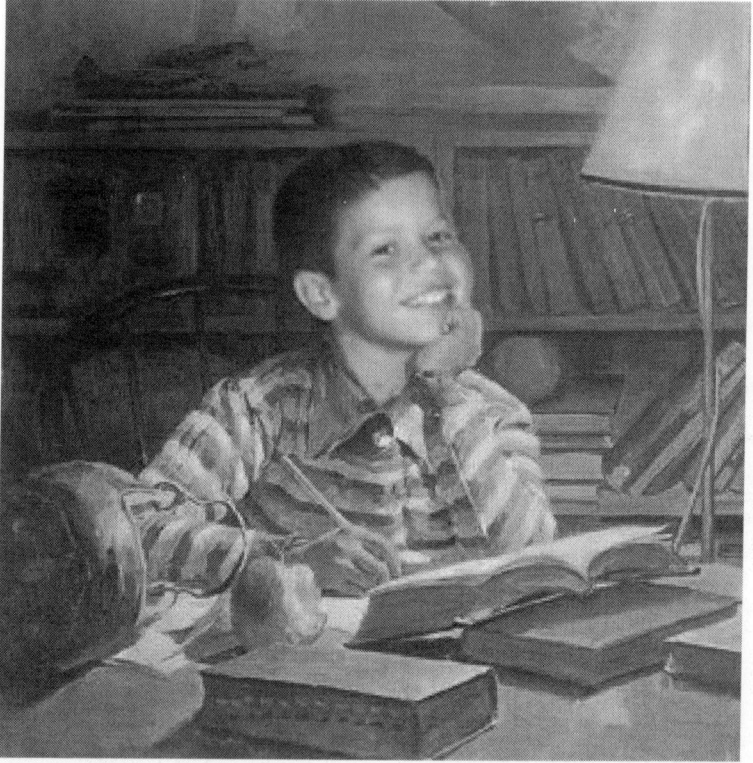

Math homework was extra tough that night. I tapped my yellow number 2 pencil on the dining room table, as I wondered how solving these ridiculously difficult math problems would ever serve any useful purpose in my life. Presently, all they were doing was infringing on my valuable television viewing time. Who cared how far apart two trains would be in forty-five minutes if they left the station and traveled in opposite directions at thirty-seven miles per hour? At age nine, I could already tell that I had no aspirations to be a train conductor, especially if it meant dealing with this kind of mathematical nonsense. I was becoming more frustrated by the minute, as I struggled with the seemingly endless barrage of complex calculations.

It had become clear to me that this tortuous assignment was part of a larger conspiracy, orchestrated by my fourth grade teacher Sister Mary Monica—a sinister plot carefully crafted to rob me of my youthful, carefree existence. There was no doubt in my mind that this assignment had been given to me in retaliation for the time I had placed pieces of chalk in the folds of Sister Monica's eraser, so that when she tried to erase the chalkboard, she was actually writing on it. Unfortunately nuns were not blessed with a great sense of humor or an appreciation for practical jokes. Sister Monica certainly had not found the humor in that one. But how had she figured out that I had been the perpetrator of that prank? Ah!

Of course, it must have been an informant that ratted me out.

As I carefully contemplated a long list of possible "stoolies", I heard a familiar knock at the door. It was my uncle Louis Spencer (or "Luis", as my dad called him), and Serafin Guevara, a family friend. It was time for the weekly ritual that had played itself out on our kitchen counter for many years.

Uncle Luis was a math teacher at the junior high school, and Serafin was an avid reader who loved to debate theories he had studied or developed himself. My dad, though he didn't have much formal education, was a whiz at math. They would gather weekly over a cup of coffee to debate a multitude of topics, ranging from the laws of physics, to politics, to unexplained phenomena. Shortly after their arrival, one of them would introduce the topic "de jour", and the great debate would commence for the evening.

The aroma of fresh coffee permeated the house as I sat in the next room, pencil in hand, diligently pretending to do my math homework. I listened attentively to the theories and mathematical formulas being bounced back and forth, like tennis balls in a Wimbledon match.

Luis Spencer and Arnoldo Cuellar, circa 1965

For example, Uncle Luis would reach for an apple out of the fruit bowl and say, "Okay, so this is the sun, the salt shaker is the moon, and the cup of coffee is the earth. The sun is four hundred times bigger than the moon but ninety-three million miles further away, so which has the greater gravitational force on tides in the oceans?"

One evening, I remember the discussion involved drilling a hole directly through the center of the earth from one side to the other. The question was, if a marble was dropped in the hole, would it stop at the center of the earth when gravitational forces reached equilibrium, or would it continue traveling through the center due to the force of inertia? Would it continue to accelerate at thirty-two feet per second squared as it came closer to the center of the earth?

Theories about magnetic fields were discussed and drawn out on paper. Mathematical formulas and hypotheses abounded by the dozens. Calculations and diagrams drawn on coffee napkins littered the kitchen table, and pencil leads were worn to nubs. These discussions usually lasted for several hours, until there was a consensus of opinion; or, if the initial problem was solved at a decent hour, they might have moved on to a new discussion like the Bermuda Triangle, which was one of my father's favorite topics. Other times, the discussion might have been adjourned as "to be continued" another evening, over another pot of coffee.

Occasionally, when one of them proved their point and left early, my father and the remaining guest would discuss their suspicion that winner of the debate had studied up on this particular subject and cleverly introduced it into the conversation so that he would be the most knowledgeable about that evening's topic. Whether or not it was true I cannot say with any certainty, but I do know that I loved to listen to these men and their weekly deliberations as I dutifully did (or pretended to do) my homework on the dining room table in the adjoining room.

Without fail, before turning in for the night my dad would help me review my math homework and make sure that I had solved all the problems correctly. When he found a mistake, he would grab a pencil and patiently check my calculations at the kitchen counter as he pensively sipped what remained from his coffee cup.

As a result of listening to many hours of theories, formulas and calculations, I began to think that perhaps Sister Monica's motives may have been a little less devious than I had first suspected. Perhaps she knew that if I mastered these complex mathematical problems, someday I too could participate in these lively debates. Maybe she had always had more noble intentions than I had given her credit for. Was it possible that she had my best interests at heart when she gave me those incredibly difficult assignments?

Nah. I still think it was because of the erasers.

℘

As Jan and I stood over the Formica-covered breakfast counter where all of those lively mathematical discussions took place, I realized that counter must have been my father's favorite place in the whole house. It was an all-purpose workspace, where he could work on projects like repairing fishing reels to preparing tax returns. This very same counter had been the location where every December 24th, Arnoldo concocted that delicious but potent Christmas Eve punch for which he was so famous. If only that kitchen counter could talk, it would have a treasure trove of stories to tell.

8

Christmas Spirits

Christmas Eve had arrived in Benavides, and it was my father's mission to get the Coronado family in the Christmas spirit for the big bash at the Cuellar home that evening. Getting this diverse group of characters and personalities to loosen up and let their hair down required careful planning, but this task was right up his alley. You might even say that it was Arnoldo's specialty. He had a God-given talent for getting people to relax and enjoy themselves at his parties. Alright, maybe it was not all God given. He might have had a little help from Bacardi rum or Jose Cuervo Tequila, but the bottom line is that he was a great host.

He was up in the attic one morning, looking for that old string of Christmas lights that had served him well for so many years. Arnoldo had spent the morning carefully testing each bulb on the string of multicolored Christmas lights. The bloodied Band Aid on his finger was a reminder of just how hazardous the job of refurbishing the old set of lights could be. These worn and tattered old relics had given him many years of faithful service, but they were now well worn and in dire need of his help. Like a faithful old friend, he just couldn't bring himself to discard them. Why, with a little electrical tape and some old-fashioned ingenuity they could continue to add Christmas cheer to the Cuellar household for years to come. Besides, it had become a matter of personal pride with Arnoldo. No string of Christmas lights regardless of its condition would get the better of him.

He had grown up in rural Mexico, in a time and place where there were no hardware stores or no spare parts. Men prided themselves in their ability to repair things with materials at hand. No sir, a trip to the hardware store would be like waiving the white flag of surrender. He would fight this battle and take no prisoners until these red, green, yellow and blue lights were in perfect working condition.

Later that day, the crisp winter afternoon air was filled with the smell of freshly mowed grass, the driveway was neatly swept, and the newly refurbished Christmas lights proudly adorned the roof line of the Cuellar home. All was ready, so Arnoldo shifted his attention to the backyard, where he began readying the barbecue pit for the Coronado family Christmas party. He had been to the Piggly Wiggly earlier to pick up sirloin steaks.

"These steaks were mooing in the pasture just last week," Dan Redner, the butcher, had reassured him. Having worked as a butcher himself, Arnoldo knew the importance of selecting only the finest cuts of meat.

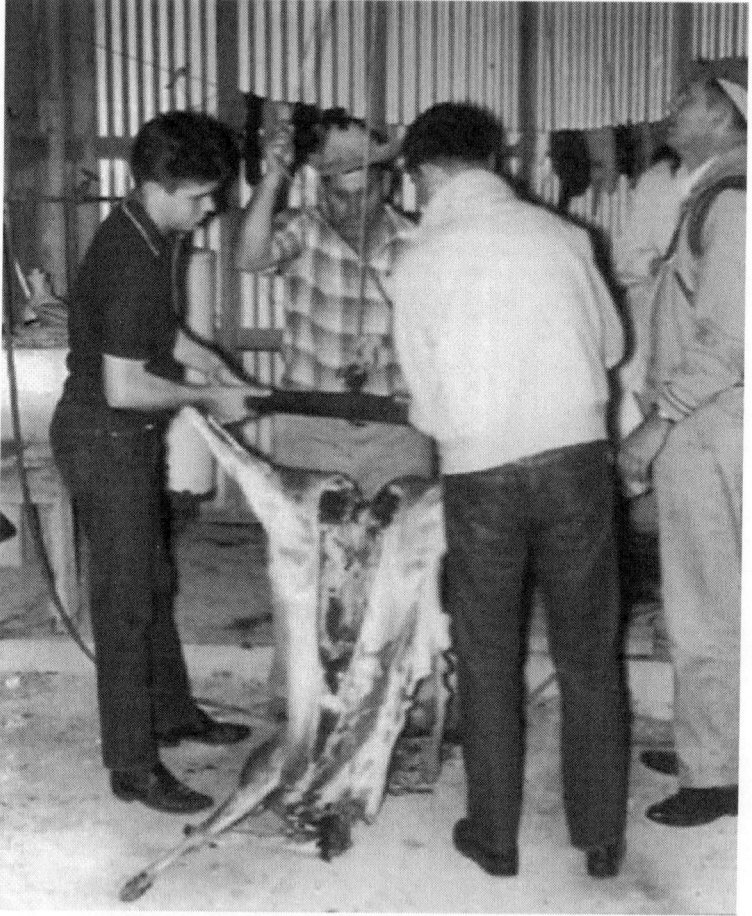

**Ruben Corkill, Paul Corkill Sr.,
Jose Coronado, Luis Spencer, circa 1960**

Paul Corkill, Arnoldo's brother-in-law, had just butchered a "cabrito" (kid goat) and dressed out a deer that his sons, Paul Jr. and Ruben, had killed at a friend's ranch. So, there would be an abundance of meat for the grill. The annual fiesta began in the backyard with the men gathered around the pit, drinking beer and discussing the town news, while the women gathered in the kitchen and prepared tamales, rice and beans, and a variety of desserts like "empanadas" (fruit filled pastries) and "pan de polvo" (Mexican wedding cookies). The hungry partygoers would consume every single one of these delicious pastries before the night was over.

Arnoldo wiped the beads of sweat from his brow with his shirtsleeve as he turned over another sizzling piece of meat on the smoky grill. His grilling job was almost done, but he was well aware that this was only the beginning of his duties for the evening. He knew that soon he would have to assume his new role as bartender when the festivities moved inside later in the evening.

Arnoldo Cuellar, 1959

If there was anything he prided himself in more than his ability as a handyman, it was his penchant for bartending. He knew that the secret to a fabulous fiesta was a perfect blend of alcohol, lively music and great food. Like Picasso was a master in oils, Arnoldo was a master in alcohol; his canvas was the punch bowl, his paints were rum, tequila, whiskey, vodka and grenadine. As for the music, a few classic Trio Los Panchos standards mixed in with some Agustin Lara classics and a few "cha cha chas" would set the perfect mood.

Being bartender at the Christmas party was tricky business. It was necessary for Arnoldo to drink his own concoctions in order to get the punch flowing, but he also had to work the crowd. Even though he had a drink in his hand the whole night, many people didn't realize that he nursed the same drink all night long. As he mingled, he carefully monitored the mood and intensity of the crowd. A lull in the crowd's noise meant that a little more rum would be added to the punch. A little too much revelry meant more pineapple juice and a little less alcohol. It was a delicate balancing act, but Arnoldo had it down to a science.

Within a couple of hours, his concoction had taken effect, and he had managed to get the crowd in the mood for dancing. At this point, many of the normally reserved members of the Coronado family had lost their inhibitions and were strutting their stuff on the impromptu dance floor in the Cuellar living room. Music blared, and the only thing higher than the spirits was the level of alcohol in the punch. Arnoldo smiled sheepishly from his perch behind the punch bowl. With a look of contentment on his face, he took another sip of punch from his cup as he surveyed the fruits of his labor on the dance floor and poured a little more rum into the punchbowl.

Irma Garcia and Jose Coronado, 1963

Guadalupe Cuellar, Macarita Young, Jose Coronado,
and Pedro Coronado on the dance floor, 1969

This whole process was not always without casualties, however. No matter how diligently Arnoldo monitored the liquor, every now and then someone got a little carried away, sometimes literally.

There was an incident one Christmas night when one of our relatives, a law enforcement officer, had over indulged in Arnoldo's punch and put on a display of macho dancing moves before passing out on the dance floor. He had to be carried off of the dance floor, holsters and pistols dragging the whole way home. This was relatively mild collateral damage, though, and no one usually suffered more than a bad headache the next day. Besides, no one ever remembered the hangovers; it was always the great Christmas party that people couldn't stop talking about.

Arnoldo loved nothing more than seeing the Coronado family enjoying each other and having a great time in his home, and to that end, his love of bar tending was only because it facilitated the process. Arnoldo passed away in 1985, and Coronado family Christmas parties were never the same without him.

Seeing my home, possibly for the last time, stirred up many fond memories. I was enjoying reliving the recollections of my past, but alas, there was work to be done. The movers had already relocated most of the large pieces of furniture to my mother's new residence in Corpus Christi, but there were many smaller items in need of packing. I decided that I would start out by packing items in the garage storage closet, while Jan boxed up items from the bedroom closets. I found the keys that unlocked the storage closets and began gathering some of the items that had been laying in storage for so many years. The first thing that caught my eye as I opened the locked closet door was my dad's old Penn Senator surf fishing reel, still sitting on the shelf where my dad had left it so many years ago. The old fishing line was still on it. As I blew off layer upon layer of the thirty years of dust that had accumulated on it, it was as if I could hear my dad's voice in the distance.

9

"La Pesca"

"Quieren ir a la pesca?" ("Do you want to go fishing?") The question emanating from my father's mouth was like sweet music to my young ears. Having grown up in this part of the world with its endless expanse of mesquite trees and flat brush land, it was always a big thrill to see the ocean. My parents and I would make that eighty-mile journey east to the sandy shores of Padre Island on the Gulf of Mexico. The beach was a wondrous place for a young boy my age. I could explore nature and expend some of the pent up, restless energy that was common among kids my age. I loved beachcombing for treasures that had drifted across the ocean and washed up on the shore. The beach was my paradise, where I could hunt for seashells, fish and camp out with my family. Of all these, fishing was my favorite.

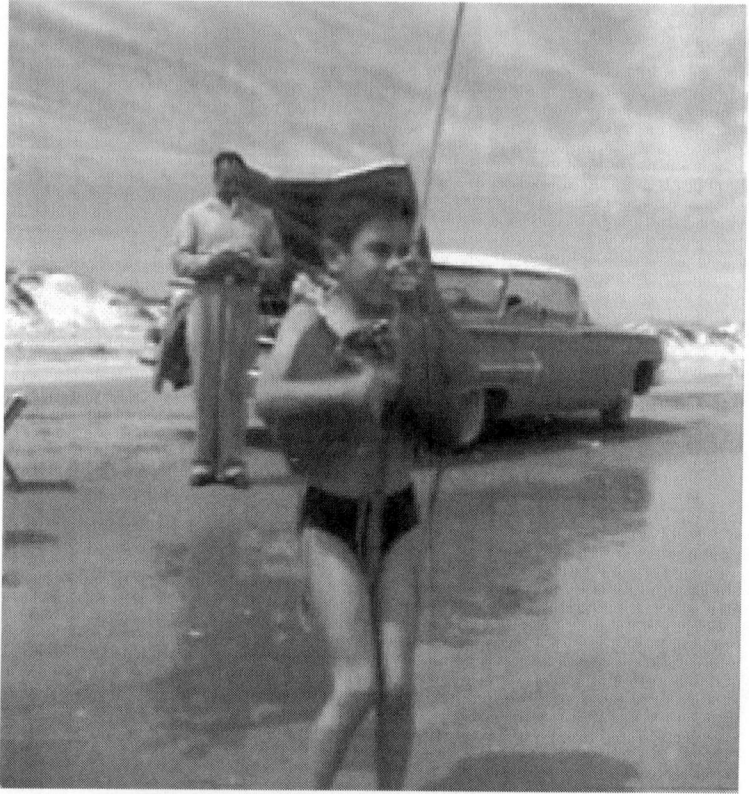

**Arnoldo Cuellar Sr. and Arnoldo X. Cuellar
fishing on the beach, 1960**

I am convinced that my grandfather Pedro Coronado had a recessive fishing gene that was most assuredly passed on to me. He had an insatiable appetite for fishing, and I must have inherited that trait because I loved it just as much as he did. While my parents both enjoyed fishing, they could never quite match our enthusiasm, or should I say, obsession for it. About once a month during the summer, we would load up the car with all the necessary gear and head out to the coast for a weekend of fishing and camping on the beach. I looked forward to these trips with all the anticipation of a kid waiting for Christmas morning.

Occasionally, my parents would let me invite one of my friends to tag along with us. This was always a treat because I enjoyed the opportunity to play the role of their outdoor guide, since I was the more experienced camper and fisherman. But most of the time it was just my parents and me, together on our weekends of adventure.

Preparations for the trip usually began early Saturday morning. My dad would begin packing all of the necessary equipment for the two-day camp out on the night before our trip. There were cots, lanterns, propane stoves, tents and fishing rods to be packed. We also needed blocks of ice so that we could keep our food cold through the entire weekend. In those days, ice was a precious commodity and not readily available at convenience stores as it is today. Procuring enough ice to last through the weekend meant taking a trip to the ice house.

Salvador Guerra, the ice man, had a small shack across the street from his Mobil service station where he stored his ice. Inside the refrigerated ice house were what from a kid's perspective seemed to be enormous blocks of ice covered by large canvas blankets, which were there for insulation. Salvador would ask to see our ice chest and then proceed to chisel out a block that fit snugly inside it.

We watched with fascination as he scored the ice with an ice pick, and with one well-placed blow of a hammer, he would separate the desired chunk of ice from the bigger block. With a mighty heave of the ice tongs, he would hoist the block and place it in my dad's aluminum ice chest that had a Pearl Beer logo on the lid.

My dad was always very careful to make sure we had enough food and supplies to last us the full two days because we would camp in a remote area of the beach, miles from civilization. The more difficult task was figuring out a way to pack all of this gear in the car. We drove a Nash Metropolitan that didn't have much storage space in the tiny trunk. But my father was a master at the art of packing. Tarps and poles were strategically strapped on the car in every configuration imaginable. Our car was quite a sight; we sometimes resembled a band of nomadic Gypsies on a caravan. Despite all of this, we always managed to arrive safely with all of our camping and fishing gear intact.

Our first stop as we arrived in Corpus Christi was Shep's Chicken Shack. Shep's was part of a local chain of drive through fried chicken restaurants. Corpus Christi didn't have any national chains like Church's or Kentucky Fried Chicken back in the 1950s and early 1960s. Shep's commercials claimed that they served up the best fried chicken in town, and they would have no argument from me. It was finger lickin' good! The wonderful thing about fried chicken was that it tasted just as good served cold as it did hot out of the fryer. We'd buy a couple of family boxes of chicken, which we could snack on throughout the weekend. The chicken was wrapped in foil and packed in the aluminum ice chest where the block ice was stored. This ice chest served as our refrigerator for the entire trip.

The final stop before we reached the campsite was always the Red Dot Bait Stand, where my dad would purchase the frozen shrimp that we would use for bait. He would buy several pounds of shrimp and carefully wrap them in a sealed plastic bag so the shrimp juice wouldn't leak in the ice chest. Finally, we were off and on our way to Padre Island, where we would camp and fish the entire weekend.

Choosing our campsite was always a difficult task, as there were about thirty miles of beach to pick from. The areas around the fishing pier were fairly crowded with beach goers and surfers. We usually wanted to get away from the throngs of beachgoers because they were a nuisance to dedicated fishermen and campers like us. We often drove ten or fifteen miles down the beach, where we would find a more secluded area with more privacy and better fishing. These more remote areas were a beachcomber's paradise. Scattered treasures abounded on the ocean's shore— everything from colored glass fishing floats to crates, barrels and enough driftwood to build a house.

My father was most in his element when he was scavenging for building materials around the beach. He loved combing the beach for old boards, driftwood and other raw materials needed to build our campsite. While my father built the campsite, I would get my fishing reel, head out into the surf and begin fishing for whiting, trout and redfish. I had to wear a life vest and wasn't allowed to go too far into the water because of the dreaded undertow that my parents always warned me about. When my father finished making camp he would come out and fish with me. I would follow several steps behind him as he waded into the surf and cast his bait into the water. I loved to fish, so I usually stayed in the water for hours until the salt water had wrinkled my skin like a dried prune—or until it was time to eat, which was the only thing I loved about as much as I did fishing.

At night, my father would build a campfire from the abundant supply of driftwood that he and I had gathered earlier. Dad would light up his propane lantern and leave it lit until late in the evening when it was time to bed down for the night. The bonfire my dad had started from the driftwood burned and crackled all night, giving us a cozy sense of security as we slept under the starry, moonlit sky. At this point, our only source of light was the dwindling campfire and whatever moonlight there happened to be.

Our family camping trips at the beach provided me with some of the most amazing experiences I can remember as a kid. At night, you could hear the soothing sound of the crackling campfire and rhythmic pounding of the surf against the sandy shore. In the darkness could be heard an occasional cry of a lone coyote howling off in the distance. Though the beach was usually a very peaceful, serene setting, I can remember one occasion when some not-so-distant intruders broke the peace.

My father always kept watch on the campsite as we slept, but by 2 or 3 a.m., he would lie down and try to catch a few winks. This one night, shortly after he fell asleep, we were all roused by the sound of someone or something making clanking sounds just outside our shelter. Tension mounted as we wondered who or what lurked in the darkness, just beyond the perimeter of our camp. Our hearts pounded wildly as my father stepped outside to confront the mysterious intruder. With a flashlight in one hand and a piece of driftwood to use as a club in the other, he proceeded to step into the darkness intending to confront the uninvited trespasser. After a few anxious moments, we were all relieved to discover that the intruders were only a couple of hungry coyotes that couldn't resist the enticing aroma of chicken bones that I had left scattered around the campsite. The excitement was over, and the mystery was solved, but I didn't get much sleep the rest of that night worrying about those pesky coyotes coming back, next time possibly for a bite out of me. I wasn't taking any chances, so I slept with one eye open for the rest of what seemed to be an endless night.

To my relief, daybreak finally came. As it did during every camping trip, daybreak brought with it the aroma of coffee and bacon cooking on the propane stove. This delightful essence signaled the beginning of the new day, filled with the promise of more exciting opportunities for a young boy to enjoy the great outdoors. Breakfast was my favorite meal. As we watched the bright orange sun rise over the splashing surf on the horizon, we would munch on bacon and egg "taquitos" that, for some reason, always seemed more flavorful on the beach. Though the food might have been a little gritty from the sandy surroundings, I can't ever remember breakfast tasting or smelling better than it did on those memorable camping trips.

The rest of the days were spent casting my line into the water, hoping to catch that one big fish that had thus far eluded my hook. My father always seemed to catch the big fish, but that didn't keep me from spending the whole day hoping my luck would change. Like Spencer Tracy in *The Old Man and the Sea*, I was out to catch that one great fish, and I wasn't giving up without giving it my best shot.

By Sunday afternoon, everyone but me was exhausted and ready to head back home. I normally pleaded with my dad to let me stay a little longer, but he usually appeased me with a promise of bringing me back another day. At this point, I usually withdrew my objection and reluctantly consented to head back home.

Perhaps it was because it signaled the end of my great adventure, or possibly because the long car ride back home was so uncomfortable, but I remember dreading the return trip home. The primitive beach campsite had no shower facilities, so we had to rinse the salt and sand off of our bodies as best we could with sea water. Though we toweled ourselves off pretty well, I could never feel really clean until I got home and took a shower. There was no air conditioning in our car, so we rode home with the windows open and the hot, humid breeze blowing in our faces. I remember how miserable the grit and sand felt on my skin for two hours on the trip home. I would try not to move a muscle because the layer of coarse sand and salt on my body felt like sandpaper rubbing on my skin. Though I can remember how much I detested the long, torturous ride back home, it must not have been too terribly bad, because I was always ready to head back on a moment's notice every time I heard my dad speak those much-anticipated words: "Quieren ir a la pesca?"

⊱

After cleaning out the garage closets, I shifted my attention back to helping Jan inside the house. As we worked our way to the living room, it became apparent very quickly what would be our packing challenge for the day. My mother had been a teacher for over forty years and had saved every textbook she had ever read, including the textbooks from her college days at Our Lady of the Lake College in San Antonio. She had a passion for literature, as evidenced by the bulging bookshelves that surrounded her home. She had instilled this love of literature in many of her students, and before she retired, she was known as one of the best educators that the Benavides school system had ever produced.

Her passion for books was matched only by her interest in collecting angel figurines. She had a menagerie of nearly a thousand angels, which she had collected over the years. Mother had started the collection herself, but it snowballed out of control because every student, friend and relative knew about her collection and, therefore, knew exactly what to give her on special occasions and birthdays. Between the angels and books, we would have a full day of packing to do.

With hands on her hips and eyes in a panoramic scan of the room, Jan assessed the monumental task before us. "I don't think we have enough tape to wrap the angels and seal all of the boxes," she proclaimed. When it came to matters of packing, Jan was the expert, so I dutifully jumped in the car and headed to the Kwik Pantry convenience store to find some masking tape.

One block before arriving at the Kwik Pantry, off to the right, I could see the old house where my maternal grandparents Pedro and Otila Coronado once lived. With Otila's nurturing hands and Pedro's ability as a provider, the two of them helped fashion the lives of a diverse group of characters known as the Coronado family. Pedro and Otila were the nucleus of the family, and without a doubt, the needle and thread that held the fabric of the Coronado family together.

10

Ma Tila's Magic and For Pete's Sake

Otila Coronado, circa 1935

Otila Coronado was one of the most fascinating and inspirational characters to grace the Coronado legacy. She was the oldest of five children born to Jose and Macaria Garza in 1902. Despite having a very limited formal education, she was thrust into the role of mother for her three sisters and one brother at the age of nine, after her mother Macaria passed away in 1911 from complications during childbirth. After courageously helping her father raise her four siblings, later in life she successfully managed to raise seven children of her own. Through much personal sacrifice and an uncanny ability to stretch a meager budget, she saw to it that all seven of her children earned college degrees. This was her dream, and she never lost sight of her conviction that education would be of paramount importance to her children's chance of success in the world.

It was in no small measure due to her unrelenting determination, single mindedness of purpose, and unwillingness to compromise this dream that she made education the centerpiece of Coronado family values. This was undoubtedly the crowning achievement of her life, and the ripple effects have shaped many of our lives and those of generations of Coronados to come.

If one had searched for the best home cooking in all of Benavides, one need not have looked any further than Ma Tila's kitchen. I can personally attest to this because I ate many a delicious meal at her table when I was growing up. Both of my parents worked, so Ma Tila would take care of me in the afternoons after school.

We had an ideal arrangement. She loved to cook, and I loved to eat anything she prepared. My favorite Ma Tila meal was "merienda". A merienda is a traditional afternoon snack with its cultural origins in Spain. Since supper in Spain is usually served late in the evening, a merienda serves to fill the gap between lunch and supper. Every afternoon around 3:30 or 4 p.m., Ma Tila would roll out some dough, season it with anise or cinnamon, sprinkle a little sugar on top of it, and place it in the oven. The two of us would munch on these delicious pastry snacks in the afternoons as we lounged on the patio furniture on her front porch.

The afternoon sun was usually blistering hot, so she would get out her garden hose and water down the concrete slab on her front porch to cool it from the sweltering afternoon heat. The evaporation cooled the porch so that we could both sit and swing on her big outdoor glider chairs. Ma Tila would sit and read her Spanish magazines while I feasted on her delicious pastries. Sometimes she would just sit and pray her daily rosary, while I ate.

"Santa Maria madre de dios, llena eres de gracia. Bendita tu eres entre todas las mujeres..." (Hail Mary full of grace, the Lord is with thee. Blessed art though amongst women...) What a terrific way for a kid to spend a hot South Texas afternoon.

Another of Ma Tila's many talents was her near supernatural ability to heal the sick. Ma Tila had developed a cure for common ailments like colds and fevers years before scientists had even ventured into this field of research. The treatment consisted of "una frotada de Vicks" (a chest slathering of Vicks VapoRub) and a dowsing with a mystical concoction composed of alcohol and various medicinal herbs that she kept in a glass bottle. This regimen was followed by a prayer to San Martin de Porres, her "go to" saint. She might on occasion petition another saint depending on the specific malady. No matter what, within a matter of minutes, whomever she treated was already feeling much better. I'm not sure if it was the Vicks VapoRub, the herbs in alcohol or the prayer, but no self-respecting illness was any match for Ma Tila's home remedy. For particularly persistent malaise, she might sit next to you and pray her daily rosary just for good measure. The results were truly amazing.

Ma Tila, in addition to all her other talents, was a shrewd businesswoman, and I credit her with having invented the garage sale. She always had an inventory of household goods, embroidery, and knick-knacks lined up on a table in her garage. There was usually a steady stream of friends and neighbors that would drop by to purchase Ma Tila's garage sale treasures. I can remember sitting in on these bargaining sessions as a child and listening in amazement as Ma Tila negotiated a sale. Ma Tila was always fair in her bargaining, but like Donald Trump, she understood the "art of a deal". The proceeds from the sale of these items were used to help stretch her usually tight household budget.

Ma Tila had an almost inexplicable interest in reading crime magazines from Mexico. I can remember seeing her buy these tabloid magazines at "el parian" (the market), on our frequent trips to Nuevo Laredo, Mexico. They contained some of the most graphic, gruesome photographs of mutilated corpses and crime victims that you have ever seen.

"Ay Dios mio!" ("Oh my God!"), she would shriek as she turned the next page to reveal another grisly crime scene. Because of her kind and nurturing ways, I found it difficult to understand her almost morbid fascination with these gory magazines. As I grew older, I came to realize that these magazines probably only served to bolster her belief that "evil" was lurking around every corner, seeking whom it might next devour. Ma Tila believed that one must be ever vigilant against evildoers or expect to be victimized just as these poor unsuspecting souls in the magazines had been. This was a theme she constantly preached to her siblings, children and grandchildren. A graphic picture was worth a thousand words of caution. Having raised her siblings as well as her own children, she understood the importance of preparing them to face the dangers of the outside world.

For a woman with very little formal education, who spoke only a few words of English, Ma Tila was without a doubt the person who had the most profound and lasting impact on the development of the Coronado family. She was a kind and caring woman, but unrelenting in her expectations of success for her children and grandchildren. Ma Tila passed away in 1973, but her venerable spirit still enriches all of our lives.

Pedro Coronado

My grandfather, Pedro Coronado, was known by more nicknames than any other member of the

Coronado family: Pedro, Pete, Pa Peyo, Pa Pedro, Payanne, Pannie, El Negro.

Pedro was born in 1896 in Laredo, Texas. At age thirteen, he became an apprentice for a mechanic in Laredo named Mr. Applewhite. It was there that he sharpened his mechanic skills, learning to repair all types of gasoline and diesel engines.

One fateful day, Mr. Archer Parr, a wealthy man known in the county as "The Duke of Duval", had car trouble while on a trip to Laredo. He arranged to have Mr. Applewhite's shop make the necessary repairs. Old man Archer was one of the few people who owned an automobile in Benavides, so needless to say, there were no automobile mechanics in Benavides at the time. Old man Archer was so impressed with Pedro's mechanical abilities that he offered to help Pedro set up his own mechanics business in Benavides. The idea intrigued Pedro, so he thought about it for a few weeks and finally decided that he would take the opportunity to move to Benavides and start up a mechanic business for himself.

With a loan he secured from Pancho Vaello, the owner of the Merchants Exchange Bank in

Benavides, he set up what could best be described as a shade tree mechanic operation. The business consisted of a small shack and a winch attached to an A-frame, which he used to hoist up motors so that he could repair them. Since there were precious few automobiles in town at that time, he learned how to repair oilfield pump jacks and other pieces of industrial equipment. He managed to keep himself busy until there were enough automobiles in town to allow him to set up his own auto repair shop.

His business grew quickly. He eventually opened Coronado Motor Company, where he did automotive repairs and sold Studebaker automobiles. Not long after this, he acquired a Gulf Oil distributorship and opened up a Gulf Oil filling station, as well. It was not long before a host of colorful characters made the service station their daily watering hole, and Coronado's Garage became a permanent fixture in the community.

**Coronado's Garage wrecker
in a downtown parade, circa 1940**

His cronies called him "El Negro", and it wasn't until I started researching his life that I discovered why. It seems that when Pedro went to work for Mr. Applewhite in Laredo, he learned much of his English from the truckers that frequented the repair shop. Many of these truckers were African American men, and Pedro, being the curious character that he was, began trying to strike up conversations with them. In the process, Pedro picked up some of the unique dialect and colorful expressions that were common in African American vernacular. His friends constantly needled him about the English he had learned from them, which is where the nickname "El Negro" came from. If it bothered him, he never let on. He actually spoke better English than most in town and he used it to his advantage in setting up his business and making friends.

Coronado's Garage, as it later came to be known, was a regular stop for many of Pedro's friends and family. Many of his friends gathered there to swap tall tales, but Pedro, being a master storyteller himself, wielded spirited tales of his own that were difficult to top.

He often told the story of one hot summer day at Coronado's Garage when a black Model A Sedan pulled up to the gas pump. In it was a man in a dark suit with an attractive young woman sitting next to him. They gassed up, went inside, paid the bill and left as quickly as they had appeared. He swore that he later recognized them from a newspaper picture, discovering that the mysterious couple was none other than the infamous Bonnie and Clyde. They must have stopped by to gas up while on their much-publicized nationwide crime spree. He told the story with such enthusiasm and vivid detail that it was hard to doubt its authenticity. But then again, it was hard to doubt any of his stories.

Pedro loved to fish and often took me fishing with him. I can remember fishing with him from the shore under the Harbor Bridge in Corpus Christi. He and I would fish for hours and usually catch a few small perch, most of which we would release back into the bay. Occasionally, we would catch a fish that was large enough to keep. We would pack it in an ice chest and take home for Ma Tila to cook. Later, I remember hearing him recount the story of our fishing trip to his friends at the service station. He told them stories of the fish we had caught, and I could hardly believe that he was talking about the same trip I had been on. My parents joked that Pa Pedro's fish kept growing even while they were in the freezer.

Pedro married Otila Garza, and together they raised seven children: Lupe, Bertha, Pedro Jr., Macarita, Gloria, Jose, and Ernesto. Pedro was a remarkably dedicated worker and a very successful entrepreneur. He built Coronado's Garage into a flourishing business that provided the financial resources for all seven of his children to obtain college degrees. Pedro passed away in 1976 and left us with the wonderful legacy of Coronado's Garage, which he had successfully managed for almost fifty years. His colorful storytelling abilities were passed on to his youngest son Ernesto, who carried on this family tradition.

ॐ

We began sifting through the items one by one so that we could label the boxes they would be packed in. In the back corner of the closet was the old Bell and Howell 8mm home projector that my Uncle Ernesto had sold to my parents years ago.

Ernesto was a gadget fanatic and loved to purchase the latest in photographic equipment. He had bought a motion picture camera and projector when he went off to the army. It had been his pride and joy for many years, but one day he was a little short on cash and therefore sold the camera and projector to my mother. My mother explained to me that after a short time she gave it back to him because she knew how much he loved it and felt guilty about taking it from him. Well apparently Ernesto was again in need of money one day, so my mother bought it from him a second time. After repeated purchases of the same camera, my mother finally decided she would keep it, since she had paid for it several times over.

11

High Anxiety

Ernesto, or Neto, was the youngest son of Pedro and Otila Coronado. He was undoubtedly one of the most colorful characters in the Coronado clan, a group with no shortage of vibrant, colorful personalities. It would be safe to say that when God created Neto, he used all of the colors on his palette. He used broad heaping strokes of reds, yellows, greens, and maybe even dreamed up a few new colors especially for Neto.

As is often the case with characters like him, Ernesto gravitated towards mischief at a very early age. His unconventional way of thinking seemed to draw him into trouble like a bug drawn to a bright light.

Ma Tila, his mother, worried about Neto because even though he was a smart kid, he was not a very dedicated student and therefore often struggled with his grades. Ma Tila monitored Neto's grades closely, so one day when he returned home after taking an important exam, she was waiting for him at the door.

"¿Como te fue con el examen?" ("How did you do on the exam?")

Neto, being ever the optimist and a master of positive spin, looked at her and proclaimed, "Mama, hasta me sobraron puntos. Hice un 72." ("Mother, I even had points to spare. I scored a 72.")

How could you argue with that kind of logic and positive thinking? Ma Tila was totally disarmed when it came to Neto, and although he caused her much worry and consternation in her lifetime, because of his colorful nature, he was always one of her favorites.

I'll never forget the story about one of the times when Neto, as a young boy, got himself into some mischief. Ma Tila was at her wits end, ready to spank him, but he had hidden where she couldn't find him. His sisters, Berta, Lupe, Macarita, and Gloria, knowing that Neto always seemed to escape punishment, were more than willing to help Ma Tila locate him. Luckily they knew one of his weaknesses. They knew that Neto wouldn't be able to resist answering a popular riddle that was on the radio at the time. The riddle was in Spanish and went like this:

"Lana suve y lana baja. ¿Que es?"

As is often the case with riddles, the answer was stated in the question. The answer was "la navaja," which was a play on words in Spanish. Well, Neto being the character that he was always liked to give his own peculiar answer, which was "Orange Crush". I'm not sure why exactly—other than the fact that Orange Crush was a very popular soft drink at the time—but every time he heard the riddle he would loudly yell out "Orange Crush!"

and then burst into laughter. Well, this would prove to be his undoing on this day because the girls, knowing that Neto was hiding somewhere in the house, decided to call out, "Lana suve y lana baja. ¿Que es?" There, from under the bed where he was hiding, came Neto's answer: "Orange Crush!" Neto had been located, doomed by his own peculiar sense of humor.

Later in life, Neto enlisted in the army and was stationed in Panama. Pedro and Otila worried a lot about him and regularly sent him money for his personal needs. They later learned that Neto had been loaning this money to other people, particularly friends who would come to him with sob stories about needing to travel back home to see their girlfriends or sick relatives, or to cover gambling losses they had incurred. Needless to say, Neto was much loved by all of his friends, but Ma Tila didn't realize until much later that Neto's whole platoon was benefitting from her generosity.

The fact that so many people loved Neto despite his quirks and flaws was evidence of his charismatic nature. He sure had a way with people, which I believe is captured in this story of an event that occurred when Neto was working at the VA hospital.

The telephone rang once, then twice, and on the third ring he answered.

"Hello, Ernesto Coronado here."

The agitated voice on the other end said, "Mr. Coronado, this is VA hospital security. We have a situation here, and we may need your help."

"Okay," Ernesto responded quizzically. "What can I help you with?"

"We have one of your employees up on the old radio tower. He's been drinking, and he's threatening to jump. We've got some men down on the ground, but he says that he'll jump it they go up after him."

"Who is the guy?" Ernesto inquired.

"He says that his name is Zeke Rodriguez. Do you know him?"

"Yeah, he works with laundry services. Give me a minute. I'll get my jacket, and I'll get on over there. Tell your guys not to do anything till I get there."

"Okay, you got it, Mr. Coronado."

Ernesto grabbed his jacket and walked hurriedly to his car, started it up and navigated the narrow road to the old radio tower. He was thinking to himself, "What the hell have I gotten myself into now?"

After a few minutes, he arrived at the scene and saw the crowd gathered around the tower with their eyes raised up to the sky. An officer walked up to Ernesto's car. "See him up there," as he pointed his finger to the sky at the top of the radio tower. "Do you think he'll jump?" he inquired of Ernesto.

"Nah!" said Ernesto, shaking his head as he reached for his sunglasses. "He may slip and fall off, but I don't think he'll jump. He's just had a few beers and needs to blow off a little steam. Haven't you ever had one of those days when you've wanted to climb up there yourself?"

"Nope, not me," the officer answered smugly.

"I have," answered Ernesto. "Once he sobers up a little, he'll realize just where the hell he is, he'll look down at the ground, it'll scare the sh*t out of him, and then he'll come on down. I'm going up to talk to him."

Ernesto put on his leather work gloves so he could hold the rails as he climbed the narrow rusted metal latter that led to the top of the tower. About half way up the ladder, he looked up and yelled. "¿Oye Zeke, que estas haciendo?" (What are you doing, Zeke?).

Ernesto figured that Zeke might feel a little less intimidated if he spoke to him in Spanish. Zeke responded, "Me va a dejar mi vieja y me voy a matar." (My old lady is going to leave me, and I'm going to kill myself.)

Ernesto decided it was time to diffuse the situation with a little bit of humor, so he shouted back, "Wait a minute, Zeke, I just bought this new jacket, and I don't want to have to clean up all that mess you are going to make down there." He forced out a chuckle to try to loosen up the tense situation and climbed the rest of the way up to Zeke. Zeke was momentarily distracted from any thoughts of jumping, as he started to carry on a conversation with Ernesto.

Neto's terrific sense of humor and engaging personality could disarm almost anyone. Zeke was no exception, and Neto soon had him laughing at his jokes and the hilarious stories he was recounting.   After about thirty minutes of humorous conversation, Zeke was totally distracted and maybe a little less intoxicated, so Neto decided it was time to end the tense situation.

With a smirk on his face, he looked at Zeke, eyeball to eyeball. "Oye, Zeke, si no nos bajamos de aqui, se nos va llevar la chin*ada. No se que vas a hacer tu, pero yo me voy a bajar." (Loosely translated: Zeke, if we don't get down from here, we are going to get both of our asses killed. I don't know about you, but I'm getting down.)

As Neto began his slow descent down the rusted metal ladder, he heard a distant voice call out, "¡Esperame!" It was Zeke asking Neto to wait for him.

Neto was happy to oblige, and he helped Zeke climb down the old radio tower until he was safely to the ground. Somewhere in the middle of that thirty-minute chat with Neto, Zeke had found the courage to face his problems and the will to go on with his life. Or maybe he had just sobered up a little and seen the ground below, as Neto had predicted. In either case, it didn't matter. Zeke was down safely, and Neto was a hero.

The following week, at the staff meeting, Ernesto received an award from his supervisors for service above and beyond the call of duty. All the recognition and attention that this award had brought him didn't faze Neto. All of these accolades paled in comparison to the pleasure he would receive from recounting the story about the humorous banter between him and Zeke while their lives were literally hanging by a thread. Zeke remained forever indebted to Neto, and Neto had a new story to add to his already extensive repertoire of unique life experiences.

Neto loved to make his friends and relatives laugh. Whether it was with a joke or a comical story, he told it with such animation and enthusiasm that you hung on every word. Because he was such a gifted storyteller, it didn't matter how many times you had heard him tell it—it only got better with time. Ernesto Passed away in 1996, but his memory and his colorful stories live on. I wonder how my Uncle Neto would feel if he knew that now, he is the subject of a few of my stories.

ℌ

I was in luck. I had managed to find the last roll of masking tape in town at the Kwik Pantry convenience store. Since that was only remaining gas station in town, I decided that I had better fill up my tank. As I removed the gas cap from my tank, I happened to glance across the street, and parked on the side of the road was an old, familiar sight: "el frutero" (the fruit man).

He had been a familiar sight in Benavides ever since I was a kid. There had always been a "frutero" who drove around the neighborhoods selling fruits and vegetables from the back of his pick-up truck. My mother knew his schedule and often posted me in the front yard to keep an eye out for him when she was in need of tomatoes, onions, bananas or bell peppers.

The "frutero" purchased his fruit and vegetables at the farmers' markets in San Antonio or the Valley. He would travel from one small town to another selling his produce. His prices were generally much lower than those of the grocery stores, and with the convenience of home delivery, his services were in high demand. If a customer purchased several items, he would usually give them a "pilon", which is a gratuity given by a vendor, usually in the form of an extra item at no additional charge. Today I could see that the "frutero" had his truck half filled with watermelons.   South Texas watermelons were some of the sweetest I ever tasted, and seeing them reminded of the times as a kid when my Uncle Paul Corkill and I used to pick them from the fields out in the countryside.   Uncle Poo, as we called him, was married to my mother's sister Bertha. He was quite a character.

12

Poo's Great Watermelon Heist

It was a mid-July summer day in the farm and ranch country surrounding Benavides. The azure, mid-morning sky looked even bluer than usual with only a few wispy white clouds brushing against the sweltering hot sun. I mopped the beads of sweat from my forehead with the sleeves of my shirt as my eyes scoured the sandy red earth for a glimpse of a big one. At last, there it was, the object of my quest: a thirty-pound, plump, Black Diamond watermelon. With my Uncle Paul's pocket knife in hand, I bent over my prize, hoping to separate the large, green, succulent treasure from its long, stringy vine, when—"Ouch!"—a sudden sharp pain in my ankle froze me in my tracks. Having grown up in the brush country, I was no stranger to the piercing bite of South Texas grass burrs. I quickly dropped the prized fruit back to the ground as I reached for my ankle with my free hand, when off in the distance I heard a voice, "¡Oyes huerco cabron! No hay tiempo para sacarte los cadillos." ("Hey *%#*~*% kid! There's no time for removing grass burrs.")

It was my Uncle Paul, who also had a real knack for stringing together some very expressive expletives. He was sitting behind the wheel of the big orange and blue Coronado's Garage Gulf tanker truck. As I hurriedly removed the most painful grass burrs, I couldn't help but wonder why he was admonishing me for stopping to remove these thorny little devils that were causing me such misery. All this fuss about me stopping to remove grass burrs just didn't make a whole lot of sense to me. After all, Uncle Paul had reassured me that the farmer was a friend of his, who had given us permission to take some of the emerald green striped beauties from his field. Uncle Paul certainly had his share farmer friends, so I had no real reason to doubt his explanation.

That deduction, as it turned out, was not one of the best my twelve-year-old brain had ever made. In my defense, however, you must take into account that my limited view of the outside world had been fashioned by television serials like Roy Rogers, The Lone Ranger and The Cisco Kid. In my world, the rules were simple. The good guys always triumphed over the bad guys. Maybe you can understand why I couldn't, in my wildest dreams, imagine that I might be involved in anything as sinister as watermelon thievery. After all, we were the good guys that wore the white hats, weren't we?

I removed the burrs as best I could and went on about my business gathering about a dozen more melons, which I carefully handed over the barbed-wire fence to my uncle. Paul then loaded them on the back of the tanker truck. The thought crossed my mind that Uncle Paul must have had a lot of good farmer friends because we made two or three more stops along the way to gather more watermelon from other fields. Uncle Poo told me that he would stop by to personally thank them later, so I didn't give it much more thought.

What I didn't realize until much later was that we had all the ingredients for the perfect crime. My Uncle Paul drove the gasoline distribution truck for Coronado's Garage. He distributed gasoline to the smaller surrounding rural farm communities like Concepcion, Ramirez and Realitos. Seeing the Coronado's Garage tanker truck on rural back roads was as common as seeing bugs splattered on your windshield. People didn't raise an eyebrow when they saw this big gasoline tanker on the roadside. As for the twelve-year-old boy on the side of the road, people just figured that nature called, and he needed to pee. It was the perfect cover for the perfect crime, and I was the unwitting accomplice.

"Crime" might be a little too harsh a word to describe this caper. As I grew older, I came to realize that many of my friends had been involved in the same summertime ritual and that it had become almost a rite of passage for many young boys my age. I also learned that most of the farmers expected that a certain portion of their crop, especially at the perimeter near the fences would be shared with passersby. Besides, Uncle Poo was more like a modern day Robin Hood and only kept a few for himself. He distributed the majority of the loot to friends and family, who always cherished these pilfered delights.

To this day, every time I get a grass burr on my ankle I stop and chuckle because off in the distance I can still hear, "Oyes huerco cabron!"

Paul was raised on the ranch by his father, Marty, along with a host of other cowboys and ranchers. As you might imagine, this is where Paul acquired his very colorful vocabulary and honed it to perfection. To say that he was anything less than a colorful character would be a considerable understatement. Paul was a completely unassuming man who never sought the limelight; however, with the help of a few well-placed expletives, he could certainly get his point across in any discussion. Oddly, people never seemed to take offense to his colorful expletive-seasoned homilies. As Paul's son-in-law, Jose Cisneros, would eventually state so well in Paul's eulogy, "That was just Paul's way."

Paul Corkill Sr.

Paul Corkill was the fourth generation descendent of William and Eleanor Corkill, who immigrated to America from The Isle of Man in Ireland. They arrived in Indianola, Texas (Rockport) in 1853 aboard the three-masted schooner, The Samuel Lawrence. Seeking to make a better life for themselves and their children, they moved to the coastal village of Corpus Christi. Sadly, the couple fell victim to a yellow fever epidemic that struck the region in 1854, and the two perished before the end of the year. Joseph Almond, a very generous local rancher took it upon himself to make sure that all of the children found suitable homes. He even raised several of them as his own. Paul was the great grandson of one of these children, John Corkill.

Having been raised with cowboys, it wasn't surprising that Paul became an accomplished cowboy himself. His expert roping skills were well known throughout the area; so well, in fact, that he was often called upon to rope some of the more ornery livestock that other cowboys couldn't handle. Paul never lost his love of the cowboy way of life and continued to raise horses and care for livestock for many years after he left the ranch. Poo was loved by the young kids, and nothing made him happier than hoisting one of his kids, grandkids, nieces or nephews on the back of a well-groomed horse for a photograph.

Hollis Young, John Edward Corkill

**Poo, Berta Elena Cisneros, Joey Cisneros,
Paul Cisneros, and John Edward Corkill**

Paul's other passion was cooking, especially the outdoor variety. He loved the opportunity to prepare a meal for his friends and family, and there wasn't a major holiday when you couldn't find Paul preparing cabrito, sangrita, chicharrones, or his world-class menudo, which was legendary. Coronado's Garage, which Paul operated in the 1970s, was a place where, while filling your tank with gas, you could just as easily fill your plate with one of the many tasty delicacies from Paul's grill. You might pay for the fuel, but never the meal. Needless to say, it was a place where all, including the occasional lost motorist, were welcomed, and it became a regular watering hole for Paul's many friends and relatives. Under Paul's management, Coronado's Garage was a friendly place where you could drop in and catch up with the latest news while you enjoyed Poo's tasty cuisine and his generous hospitality.

Paul died in the year 2000. His son-in-law, Jose Cisneros, gave the most eloquent account of Paul's life in his eulogy on the day of his funeral. I have included it below, it its entirety, because it captures the essence of Paul's life and legacy so powerfully.

"For those of us who loved him and those of us who knew him as a friend and neighbor, Paul Corkill does not need a eulogy, but he deserves one.

A humble and unpretentious man, he reflected the work ethic of his generation and spent his time providing for family and seeing that he improved their lives over his.

He was born in Realitos, Texas, in 1919 and spent his early years alongside his younger brother Johnny, working the Corkill ranch. In later years, he would care for him through his remaining years.

He married Berta Coronado in 1937 and eventually settled in Benavides where he himself did a little ranching while working at the local gasoline refinery. He later worked for his father-in-law and eventually operated the Coronado Garage for several years. His years as a garage operator are legend. He not only dispensed fuel, but the garage became a meeting place for all of his friends. His coffee pot was always full, and an occasional snack was often added. To the oil company motorist traveling through Benavides in those days were such travel necessary, Paul's garage was a welcome way station for fuel and food even in the early hours of the morning. He was generous to a fault.

One could describe him as something of a

character. Irreverent at times, he had a unique way of putting things in their proper prospective. His often colorful vocabulary reflected the rough upbringing of his early years. But people paid no mind. It was simply Paul's way.

He was a good husband to Berta and a good father to his children, Berta, Margot, Paul, Ruben and John. His sixty-three years of marriage to Berta has to date produced a progeny of thirty-two offspring. His five children have given them a total of fourteen grandchildren, thirteen great-grandchildren and one great-great-grandchild.

With limited education of his own, he saw to it that not only his children received a better education, but also his wife, who dropped out of school to marry him. They all made him proud. That was perhaps his life's accomplishment.

For a man who never ventured far from his roots, his children have carried the Corkill name to places of which he never dreamed. From the OPEC oil fields of Venezuela, to the inner sanctum of our national security, to the leadership of our children's education, and last but not least, to the protection and preservation of our national heritage—the Corkill name has resounded in all these places—if not the sons, then the daughters who have stood along their husbands as teammates in their endeavors.

And these are only his children's accomplishments. His grandchildren are already carving out their own goals—evidence our own Father Carroll here today. And soon it will be the great-grandchildren's time. They are ready too.

Not bad for a simple man affectionately known to his grand kids as Poo.

Despite all of this, he will be greatly missed. No longer will we have our own information center as to the goings on in Benavides.

Losing one's parents is an inevitable part of life, but often difficult to accept. Parents are the last bastions of hope in a sea of uncertainty. It is a life support that never ends. For life's lessons from our parents do not end with their passing. We will always remember Poo and everything he left us.

When death finally came, he did not go easy into that night. His strength was manifested when after all hope for his recovery was gone and all life support was removed, he continued to breathe on his own for several days until his system finally said,   'no   more.'

He died surrounded by his children and wife. And just before taking his last few breaths, he opened his eyes as if to get one last look at his family and to say goodbye.

We   will   miss   him   dearly.

But yet, one has only to look at his children to see something of Poo in all of them. And even down to his great grandchildren—evidence the lady who saw the Corkill features in our youngest grandson Cameron, when he was here with our daughter Lisa. To that end Poo will always be with us.

May God bless him and take care of him."

ဆ

As I stood there gazing at the "frutero", I thought for a moment about buying a watermelon but decided not to. I just knew that it would measure up to the exquisite flavor of those memorable treasures that Uncle Paul and I had heisted from the local melon fields so many years ago. With masking tape in hand, I secured the gas cap on my tank, climbed in the car, and decided to take a short detour by Uncle Paul's house. Even though Paul had passed away ten years earlier, his wife Bertha still lived alone in their old house on the edge of town.

I stopped in and visited with Aunt Bertha for a few minutes. We talked about old times and memories of the Easter outings we used to have at Poo's ranch out in the country. Paul had a small ranch about four miles north of town, where he raised a few cattle and horses. Every Easter Sunday, the entire Coronado clan and friends piled in their cars and headed north to Paul's ranch for the annual Easter family barbecue and picnic. It had been a tradition and was always one of the most anticipated events of the year for the entire Coronado family. Aunt Berta loved to have a cold beer in the afternoon, so she asked me to join her in a Coors Light as we fondly recalled some of the more memorable Coronado Easter picnics at Paul's ranch.

13

Spring Awakenings

Spring had just arrived in the brush country of South Texas. The ashen shades of gray that had painted the Benavides landscape for the past three months had now given way to new more vibrant colors. Nature's own shades of emerald and shamrock green now adorned the color palette of the reawakening countryside. The "agrito" (wild currant) bushes were exploding with new clusters of bright red berries, and the "nopales" (cacti) were showing off their new crimson tunas (fruit of the cactus plant) like bright new ornaments on a Christmas tree. The mockingbirds could be heard for miles around, chirping their latest compositions, and everywhere you looked, swarms of migrating black and yellow Monarch butterflies dotted the cloudless blue skies. The unmistakable sweet smells and sounds of spring filled the crisp morning air. This seasonal renewal of life served as a reminder that the annual Coronado family Easter picnic at Paul Corkill's ranch was fast approaching.

As a young boy, my thoughts were filled with great anticipation because plans were taking shape for one of the most awaited events of the year. The route to the big family celebration had been etched in our minds so well that the cars could practically navigate the route themselves. Destination five miles north on Highway 339. Turn left off the pavement at the metal gate adorned with rusty yellow sign touting the goodness of Fairmaid Bread, then one mile down the winding "caliche" road past the livestock watering pond, to the large cluster of Hackberry trees. These large trees provided the shade necessary for all of the activities and events of the much-anticipated Easter fiesta.

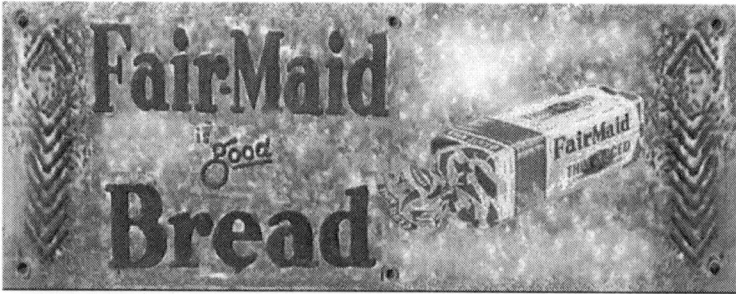

The days leading up to Easter were busy ones for everyone in the Coronado clan. As preparations for the big family picnic began, I can remember the phone lines buzzing with conversations that might have sounded something like this:

"Lupe, are you making rice for the picnic on Sunday? Berta is making the beans, Gloria is making potato salad. Mother (Ma Tila) is making capirotada (Mexican bread pudding), and Mac is bringing cakes and pies from Three Brothers Bakery in Houston."

"Do you think that's going to be enough food because the Tias from Laredo are coming, and Neto is bringing some of his friends from work."

"I don't think that food is going to be a problem. Paul is butchering a hog, cooking chicharrones (fried pork rinds) and cabeza en pozo."

("Cabeza en pozo" is a cow's head that is buried overnight in the ground on coals, with skull, eyeballs, cheeks, tongue and brains included. Hmmmm! Good!)

"Nono bought some sirloin steaks and mollejas (sweetbreads), so I think were okay on food. Remember that we're all meeting at mother's house on Saturday to make tamales."

As a kid, I never quite understood everyone's preoccupation with making a good impression on the visiting Tias (Ma Tila's sisters-in-law) from Laredo. It seemed to me that they were treated like visiting foreign dignitaries. I suspect that all the fuss must have had something to do with wanting to make sure Ma Tila looked good in the eyes of her in laws.)

For months leading up to the big day, my mother would save dozens of empty eggshells left over from breakfast, so that I could have an ample arsenal of "cascarones", which are confetti-filled eggshells that are to be cracked on the heads of unsuspecting victims. Cracking these confetti-filled cascarones on the heads of friends and family has long been a Mexican/Texan tradition, a way of celebrating Easter and the arrival of spring.

In preparation for the big Easter egg hunt, which was another Coronado family tradition, parents had stockpiled bags of pastel colored plastic eggs and mounds of synthetic green grass to hide them in. Everyone loaded their cars and pickups with Easter baskets, folding chairs, and ice chests teeming with soft drinks and beer. This convergence of family and Easter paraphernalia signaled that the annual Easter pilgrimage to Paul Corkill's ranch was now officially underway.

The preparations for the much-anticipated fiesta began on Saturday before Easter. The unmistakable aroma of "masa"—dough for the tamales seasoned with chili powder and "comino" (cumin) and "carne de Puerco" (pork meat)—filled the kitchen at Ma Tila's house, as the Coronado women arrived to begin the labor-intensive ritual of making tamales. This was truly a labor of love and the process consisted of four basic steps, and one or two people were assigned to each delicate procedure.

The first group would prepare the masa. Another group would spread the masa on the corn shucks (referred to as "embarrando"), while the next group would fill the corn shucks with ground beef and a few raisins. (Raisins were optional.) Finally, the shucks were folded and cooked. This whole process moved along with all the efficiency of a Detroit automobile assembly line. Henry Ford himself would have been impressed. The techniques had been refined by many generations of Coronado "tamaleras" (tamale makers), and this generation of Coronado women had perfected it to a culinary art form.

Otila Coronado and other Coronado tamale makers

While the women prepared the tamales on Saturday, the men were busy making preparations for the picnic at the ranch. The picnic site was located under the shady canopy of several large Hackberry trees. Wooden picnic tables were arranged underneath the trees, and the site was cleaned up in preparation for the big day.

Early one Easter Sunday, my father and I arrived at Paul Corkill's house to help Paul butcher a hog, which he would use make chicharrones. I had very mixed emotions about hog butchering. On one hand, I was thrilled to be included in the activities with grown-ups; on the other hand, I really dreaded what was coming next. I can still vividly recall watching my Uncle Paul walking up to the hog pen with his .22 rifle in hand, as I covered my ears and looked the other way. I knew all too well what was about to happen. Uncle Paul had grown up on the ranch, and the slaughtering of farm animals for food had become second nature to him. But this little four legged bundle of ham reminded me a little too much of that stuttering cartoon character Porky Pig. I couldn't bear to watch this execution. In the back of my mind, I could hear poor Porky squealing, "Th-th-th-that's all folks!" as Uncle Paul pulled the trigger.

Once the dirty deed was done, there was not much time to grieve Porky's life because it was now time to prepare the meat used to make the chicharrones. My cousins and I circled around the metal table and watched in utter amazement, with emotions that ranged from outright horror to utter disgust, as Uncle Poo and my father Arnoldo laid the hog carcass on the metal slab and began the process of cleaning up the hairy little beast. Burlap sacks were placed over the entire body, and boiling water was poured over the burlap sacks. This process was repeated until the hair and mud loosened enough that it could be swept off with a broom.

Arnoldo Cuellar, Susie Spencer, Arnoldo X. Cuellar, Paul Corkill Sr., and Ruben Corkill, circa 1960

Finally, Poo carefully dissected the meat into the different cuts: bacon, ham, roast, etc. The pork rinds (skin and belly fat) were cut into small pieces and placed into a big cast iron pot that reminded me of a witch's cauldron. The chunks were fried in lard until they were crisp, and then placed in a burlap sack. With Arnoldo holding one end of the sack, and Poo the other, they twisted each end in opposite directions until most of the grease was squeezed from the chicharrones. They were fresh out of the pot, finger-lickin' good, and now ready to be sampled. You haven't lived until you have treated your taste buds to the flavor of one of these delicious little artery-clogging appetizers.

Late in the afternoon came time to start preparing the aforementioned "cabeza en pozo" (cow skull, with brains, eyeballs, etc.). Since this tasty delicacy had to cook overnight, the men started the process of building the fire that would provide coals needed to prepare it. A large pile of mesquite wood was stacked on the ground, and the fire was lit.

The pungent—almost intoxicating—aroma of burning mesquite wood filled the crisp evening air. An orange glow tinted the darkening evening sky as men and boys gathered around the flickering fire. I know this because I was one of those young boys who listened in wide-eyed amazement and hung on every word as the men discussed local politics, the weather, and spun tall tales. I soaked it all in and believed every word as the gospel truth.

In preparation for the "cabeza en pozo", the men would dig a hole about 3-feet-deep by 2-feet-wide. At the bottom of the hole, a layer of burning embers and hot coals was shoveled in. The head of the cow was seasoned, wrapped in foil, and then placed in a 5-gallon size lard can. The can would be lowered into the hole and covered by a sheet of corrugated aluminum. A heavy layer of fiery coals was then placed on top. By morning, the meat was cooked to perfection and ready for sampling. Yum!

As a young boy, there was no greater thrill than to be asked to somehow participate in the mostly adult-dominated picnic preparations. Most of the time it involved just riding shotgun with my older cousin Paul Jr., as he returned to town for more picnic supplies from the Cash Store or the local Piggly   Wiggly.

I have memories of one such trip in the late 1950s, when Paul Jr. and I piled into Poo's old green Ford F-100 pick-up truck and headed into town for supplies. Down the winding dirt road we went, a white plume of caliche dust rose over the tree line in our wake. Our heads bobbed up and down as we navigated the ruts and craters on the tortuous ranch road. Blaring on the radio was Paul's favorite song of 1959, "The Battle of New Orleans" by Johnny Horton. Paul Jr. would turn up the volume on the radio and burst out into almost hysterical laughter when the song came to the part that said:

"We fired our cannons 'till the barrel melted down, so we grabbed an alligator and we fought another round. We filled his head with cannon balls and powdered his behind, and when we touched the powder off, the gator lost his mind."

The tune was the number one song of 1959, and, no doubt, Paul Jr. thought that this was the best song ever written. And, you know what? I probably have to agree with him because we laughed all the way into town and it became a priceless boyhood memory. To this day, I still think of Paul Jr. and our great adventure every time I hear the song on the radio. Paul Jr. passed away in 2010. His infectious sense of humor, love of family, and his reverence for family history and traditions will be greatly missed.

14

An Uninvited Guest

It was 10 a.m. in the small South Texas town of Benavides, and Easter Sunday services had just ended. The congregation poured out of St. Rose of Lima Church and milled outside the entrance, exchanging pleasantries as they admired all of the well-dressed children in their new Easter outfits. A noticeable sense of excitement filled the air, as parishioners waited outside to greet Father Santa Maria. Men, women, and children posed for Easter photographs at the church entrance as they conversed about plans for their Easter family gatherings and picnics.

Father Santa Maria and the Coronado Family

It was a glorious spring day, the kind of day that God might have handpicked for just such a special occasion. Now that church service had ended, a parade of Coronado family vehicles made its way to Paul Corkill's ranch in the mesquite brush country, five miles north of Benavides. The aroma of mesquite smoke and meat on the grill seemed to filter through the entire picnic area under the large Hackberry trees. There was an air of great anticipation as family and guests had arrived with all their folding chairs and Easter paraphernalia in hand.

The young children, now energized by the consumption of large quantities of sugar from Easter candies and chocolate eggs, ran around wildly with their Easter baskets in hand. All of the excitement was in anticipation of the big Easter egg hunt, which was usually the highlight of the Easter picnic. Picnic tables were full of family and friends, who had come together for a day of celebration. Fun, food, and frolicking were to be the order of the day.

Susie Spencer and her Easter Basket

Every year Father Santa Maria, the local parish priest, would pull up in his black Ford Falcon to join in on the fun. It had been a long-standing tradition with the Coronados to include the Parish priest in family celebrations like these. Father Santa Maria always enjoyed sharing part of his Easter Sunday with the family. Though, he couldn't stay very long because of other commitments, he always made it a point to make an appearance and share a meal with the Coronados.

Father Santa Maria

Father Santa Maria was quite an enigmatic figure. He was a deeply religious man of the cloth, steeped in the old traditions of the Catholic Church from his native Spain, but also a man with a dichotomous nature, to say the least. On one hand, he preached the gospel of Jesus from his Bible, but on the other, he could go toe-to-toe with Paul Corkill in an expletive-laden discourse that could make a seasoned sailor blush. He often began these encounters by reminding Paul that he needed to become more involved in church activities, knowing full well that Paul would not hesitate to give his colorful reply, usually laced with a litany of expletives. Father would counter with an equally spicy rebuttal. Out of respect, Paul usually smiled, shook his head, and let Father get in the last word.

Looking back on it, I think that Father Santa Maria probably baited Paul into these conversations because he secretly enjoyed the opportunity to engage him in these earthy discussions. Like two heavy weight boxers who admired each other's knockout punch, they never lost respect for each other and remained good friends despite these occasional verbal sparring sessions. Truth be known, they probably both looked forward to the opportunity to go toe-to-toe in their next rematch. It was all in good fun, and I suppose that Father looked at this as an effective way of reaching out to communicate God's message of salvation to all the members of his flock. Or maybe he just liked the earthy language because it made him feel like a regular guy, just an ordinary sinner like the rest of us. We'll probably never know the real answer.

I recall one year when our Easter celebration took an unexpected turn. It all began normally, with Father arriving in his black Ford Falcon. He greeted family and friends and proceeded to give an abbreviated version of grace because he was a very perceptive man, and he knew not to stand between the Coronados and their food. Or maybe he was just eager to sample the tasty fare himself. In either case, he took his place of honor at the head of one of the picnic tables and proceeded to fill his plate with the many tasty offerings from the grill.

"Jose, can you pass the potato salad?"

"Here it is. Can you pass me the beans, please?"

"Mama, look at the big kitty up in the tree."

"Mijita, there's no kitty up in the tree."

"Yes, mama, look! He's smiling at us up there! Look! Look up there."

"Oh My God. Nobody move. There's a tiger up in the tree."

"That's not a tiger, it's a bobcat," came the reply from someone at the table.

"Go get Paul."

There he was, perched about 20 feet above the picnic tables on a large horizontal branch of the Hackberry tree—a full grown, South Texas bobcat. Everyone was asked to quietly and slowly back away from the tables and get in their cars, as the men decided how to deal with this uninvited guest. Ernesto ran to get his pistol from his car. Paul and Ruben went to get their rifles from the truck. The testosterone and adrenalin levels were running high as every able-bodied man with access to a gun scurried to get into position to get a good shot. After all, they felt that they were protecting innocent women and children from this deadly predator.

The fact of the matter was that we had most likely invaded the bobcat's home, and he was probably more afraid of us than we were of him, but this definitely was not his lucky day. Every man there who had ever dreamed of being John Wayne positioned himself under the tree and took dead aim at the cat. On the count of three, a barrage of lead bullets and smoke filled the air, like a scene from an old western shootout. After the smoke cleared, and the shooting stopped, the cat lay motionless on the ground. Every man with a gun claimed that his shot had been the one that had felled the dangerous beast. In reality, Paul Corkill and his son Ruben were the only ones experienced enough with a rifle to rightly claim the kill. This didn't matter, and every man who fired a shot basked in the glory of the moment. Finally, the bobcat was removed, and the area was declared safe again. The family had been saved from a grizzly fate, and the celebration continued again in full swing, minus one uninvited guest.

ॐ

Aunt Bertha and I sipped from our icy cold long neck bottles and had a few more laughs as we reminisced about the good old days. I hugged her, thanked her for the beer, and said goodbye because it was time for me to head back to my mother's house and help Jan with the packing and taping.

In the time I was gone, the angels and books had all been boxed and loaded, and most of what remained was small items and contents of the drawers from my mother's dresser. Found in the memorabilia was a cardboard box heaped full of old pictures. This one box contained much of the history of the Coronado family in pictures.

I had one uncle in particular who was fascinated by Coronado family history. My Uncle Hollis Young was married to my Aunt Macarita, whom we called Aunt Mac, and they lived in Houston. Together they built a home where everyone who entered was welcomed and made to feel like part of the family. I can attest to this, as I had the opportunity to live with them one summer when I was in high school. I have extremely fond memories of that summer. The Young's home was always a beehive of activity, and they seldom missed an opportunity to host a fiesta for the Coronado family and friends.

15

Holly Jolly Fiestas

Hollis and Macarita Young

The fiesta at the Young's house was in full swing, as family and guests filtered in. My Uncle Hollis gravitated toward his favorite location, behind the bar, standing next to his old typewriter. The bar was positioned conveniently between the kitchen and the spacious living room, where guests were conversing and enjoying the great music. It was the perfect location for Hollis because he could converse with guests in either room while he typed on his old typewriter. The rhythmic rat-tat-tat of Hollis's old manual typewriter sounded in the background, as "Sabor a Mi" by Eydie Gorme y Los Panchos fueled the festive mood of the crowd.

The blender on the bar was dripping with beads of condensation from the frozen concoction that his wife Macarita was so famous for—a splash of triple sec, lime juice, some ice cubes, and 1.5 oz. of Jose Cuervo tequila. The 1.5 oz. of tequila was just a recommendation, as far as Macarita was concerned, so she often tweaked the dosage as she deemed necessary. Hollis and Macarita both loved hosting these fabulous fiestas for their family and friends.

Hollis Young, circa 1970

Hollis Young's love for Hispanic culture was evident throughout his home, not only by his choice in music (and, of course, his choice of spouse, my Aunt Macarita), but also by the Mexican and Guatemalan artwork that he proudly displayed in his home. Everywhere you looked there were treasures of art that he had painstakingly packaged and brought back with him from his sojourns to Mexico and Guatemala. Each piece was a priceless memory from a place that he considered to be like paradise on earth. You had better pull up a bar stool and be prepared to stay a while if you ever got him started talking about his own private little corner of Eden, Lake Atitlán, Guatemala.

Lake Atitlan, Guatemala

Hollis spent countless hours at his typewriter because he was a born researcher with a passion for reading, gathering and disseminating information. He was especially fascinated by the Coronado family genealogy, which dated back to the original Spanish land grants in Mexico. He had spent many tireless hours of his time digging through baptismal and court records, as he tried to reconstruct the family lineage. This research had led him to the inevitable conclusion that somewhere along the line, one of our Spanish ancestors had charmed some fair Tlaxcalan Indian maiden, and that we, the present day Coronados, were the progeny of this relationship. I say "inevitable" conclusion because it would only take one glance at our ancestor's pictures for anyone to see our undeniable Indian heritage. As one astute family member observed, "All that is missing are the feathers." This former VA hospital administrator shall remain nameless to protect his identity.

Jose Prisciliano Coronado (1849-1894)

One day, Hollis's excitement over his genealogical discovery prompted Pedro Jr., his brother-in-law, to proclaim, "Hollis! I don't want to hear one more damn thing about those %@&*^$ Indians." Alas, I guess you can never be a prophet in your hometown, or in this case, your own family. Hollis took all of this abuse in stride and continued undaunted with his genealogical research.

Dr. Pedro Caram and Arnoldo Cuellar at Hollis Young's bar

Hollis continued his rhythmic rat-tat-tat on the typewriter keys from behind the bar, as the Coronado family and friends spread out throughout the house. One group in the living room, drinking margaritas and listening to the music, another in the kitchen, eating pastries and catching up on the latest family gossip (the "chisme" hotline, as we called it), while the younger kids played games and watched television in the back bedroom.

Besides having a marvelous time, the one thing you could always count on at a Young family fiesta was a bountiful supply of delicious food and sumptuous deserts and pastries. Everyone moved about the Young's home as if it was their own. And why wouldn't they? Many of them, like myself, had been boarders there during our summer vacations or our school years. Hollis and Macarita had generously opened up their home to many of the Coronado kids who needed a place to stay while they learned the ropes in the big city. Since many of us had come from small towns, their home had been a safe harbor for us, especially when we were starting our careers. So, we all looked at it as our home away from home.

The typewriter went silent for a second, as Hollis called out in a concerned voice, "Macarita! Has little Hollis hit tennis balls into the practice net today?"

She answered, "He hit balls for an hour this morning. He's resting right now."

"How about Georgie? Has she had her guitar lesson today?"

"Yes, her instructor says that she is doing wonderfully," Macarita replied, in a reassuring voice.

Hollis had been a world-class tennis player in his days at Cornell University, and he understood that dedication to practice was the key to being successful at anything in this world. This was a theme he constantly preached to his children.

Aunt Mac was a master of controlling Hollis's obsessive nature and high expectations when it came to his kids practicing their athletic or musical talents. She had a sedative, almost Valium-like, calming effect on Hollis's occasional near meltdowns. Reassured by Macarita that all was going according to his plan, Hollis continued his rat-tat-tat on the old typewriter.

Hollis was an attorney (landman) for Mitchell Energy, and his job required extensive research and documentation of property ownership and mineral rights. When he stood at the bar tapping on the keys of his typewriter, everyone just assumed that he was working on some important document for a big business deal. While this may have on occasion been true, more often than not, it turns out he was documenting his thoughts and observations about the people and the goings on around him. He may have been taking a newspaper comic strip and changing the characters' names to the names of people he knew, or dreaming up political slogans for his brother-in-law, who was campaigning for office. "Arnoldo Cuellar for Tax Assessor", with the slogan underneath reading, "The Only Honest Man In Duval County." Many of his censored creations were posted on the refrigerator door in the kitchen. However, he knew all too well that being an in-law in the Coronado family was much like being a criminal on probation—one false move could land him swiftly in the pen. Knowing that some family members might not see the humor in his creations, he wisely filed many of them away, never to see the light of day.

Hollis, despite his best efforts, sometimes managed to get himself in trouble with the family. It was at times like those that he relied on his shrewd sense of humor to extricate him from some rather precarious situations—like the time he said or did something to offend one of his sisters-in-law and became "persona non grata". He knew he would have to pull out all the stops to get out of the bind he had placed himself in. So, one day he showed up at his sister-in-law's house with a bouquet of flowers. Upon opening the door, he pulled the flowers from behind his back and extended them toward her, and with his eyes closed and a toothy grin on his face, blurted out, "Howz about a kiss, Lupe?" I'm not entirely sure what the response was (though I could venture a guess), but I do remember the result was that he accomplished his mission. Peace had been restored, and he was again in good graces with the Coronado family.

Hollis's love of research was only overshadowed by his zest for life and his love of the Hispanic culture. In a family with no shortage of colorful characters, Hollis clearly distinguished himself as one of the most memorable. Hollis Young passed away in 2007. We shall all miss his wry sense of humor and the rhythmic rat-tat-tat of his old typewriter.

ॐ

In addition to the photos found in my mother's dresser were dozens of old letters that people had written to my mother. For sentimental reasons, she had saved many of the letters she had received, and stored them in this box along with her photographs.

There was one particular letter that aroused my curiosity. It was a letter from Dr. I. L. Shannon D.D.S., who was Chief of Oral Disease Research at the VA Hospital in Houston. Back in the summer of my high school days, Dr. Shannon had allowed me to work as a volunteer at his VA research laboratory. He had been instrumental in helping set my life's course toward the field of dentistry. My mother had written him a letter of appreciation for his help. He had responded to her letter, so she had saved it for me to read one day. I read the letter and couldn't help but smile because it brought to mind memories of the somewhat amusing circumstances that led up to me getting this life changing job opportunity.

16

A Rollercoaster Life

**Texas Cyclone at Six Flags AstroWorld
Houston, Texas**

"The fault, dear Brutus, is not within our stars, but within ourselves, that we are underlings." Like Cassius in Act I of Julius Caesar, I am not a big believer in fate; however, I do believe that the timing and circumstances of certain events in our lives undoubtedly affect the direction in which life takes us, like a raft swept up in a whitewater current, setting us on a course that leads us to our destiny. Whether these are events that are random occurrences, part of some cosmic master plan, or cryptically encoded in the tea leaves, I cannot say; but I have no doubt that the events and circumstances that led to my second summer job thrust me into the wake of one such life defining moment.

My first summer job, as a mere brat, had been a short stint at Coronado's Garage as a service station grease monkey. I had learned many valuable life lessons about life and about interacting with humanity in a confusing new world that I was totally unprepared for—a world in which I had many more questions than I had answers.

At age seventeen, my parents thought it was time that I start considering my career possibilities, so they suggested that I look around for a summer job. Since my Aunt Macarita and Uncle Hollis lived in Houston, they offered to let me live with them for the summer if I could get a summer job there. This sounded like a great idea to me. I had visions of working at a place like Six Flags AstroWorld. I had been there several times and had seen many high school aged kids having a great time while working at the park. I could easily picture myself eating candy and hotdogs all day while taking tickets for the Texas Cyclone rollercoaster or one of the many other exciting amusement park rides. Sounded like the perfect summer job for me. "Count me in," I thought to myself.

Well, sometimes reality has a nasty way of reaching out, biting you in the butt, and bringing you back down to earth. All these grandiose visions of my dream summer job at AstroWorld were extinguished in the time it took to make two phone calls.

It probably went something like this.

Ring, ring.
"Veteran's Administration Hospital, Assistant Director's Office, Debbie speaking, how may I direct your call?"

"This is Guadalupe Cuellar. I would like to speak to the assistant director, Mr. Coronado. Please tell him his sister is calling."

"Please hold." ….

"Mr. Coronado, I know you asked not to be disturbed, but there is a Guadalupe Cuellar on the phone who says she's your sister. Do you want me to put her through?"

Jose Coronado, for one brief moment, considered not taking the call because he was immersed in calculations for the upcoming year's hospital budget; but just as he was about to tell Debbie to take a message, the line from Humphrey Bogart in *Casablanca* echoed in the back of his head, "You'll regret it. Maybe not today. Maybe not tomorrow, but soon and for the rest of your life." Bogart's words of wisdom had come to him almost in the form of a vision. Enlightened by this brief cinematic flashback, he was now painfully aware that Coronado women, especially his sisters, didn't like to be ignored. So, he wisely decided to take Lupe's call.

"Yes, Debbie, put her through."

"Jose, I hope you weren't too busy," Lupe said.

"No, Lupe, I was just sitting here trying to figure how to get five million dollars' worth of hospital improvements done on a three million dollar budget." (His eyes rolled to the back of his head with a barely discernible hint of sarcasm in his voice.) "What's going on?"

"I just wanted to ask if you thought you might be able to help find a summer job for Arnoldo at the VA in Houston. We're trying to help him decide on some sort of career in the science field. I know that you sometimes have summer jobs available there at the hospital."

"Lupe, let me just tell you that I can't get him a paying job because there are rules against hiring relatives, but I'll try to see if I can find a volunteer job for him. Give me a few days, and I'll get back to you."

Jose was a very intuitive man, and he knew that any request from Coronado woman (especially his sisters) that began with "I was wondering if you might be able to...." was an encrypted code for "you had better get off your duff and come through with some results." So he picked up the phone and made another call.

"Dental Research Laboratory, Dr. Shannon's office, Leslie speaking."

"Leslie, this is Jose Coronado. "Can I speak to Dr. Shannon?"

"Yes, let me put you through to him."

"Hi, Jose, this is Ira. I'm glad you called. I've been meaning to call you. I guess you know about all the problems we've had with that old air conditioning system we have here in the lab. We've had problems with it all year, and it's getting worse every day. I think it's about time we replace it, and I'd like to see a new air conditioning system funded in the upcoming budget. I just wanted to put in my pitch for it. Anyway, what can I help you with?"

"Well, Dr. Shannon, I was wondering if you might be able to use a volunteer lab technician on your research team this summer. I know you already have three dental students working for you, but I have a seventeen-year-old nephew who would like volunteer if you could use him. By the way, congratulations. I heard you just got that grant from NASA to develop an ingestible toothpaste for the astronauts."

"Thanks, Jose. I've got a good team here, and you know that you can count on me to make room for your nephew. Consider it done. By the way, Jose, what do you think my chances are of getting that new air conditioning unit for the lab in next year's budget?"

"Well, Dr. Shannon, I promise you I will do my best to get your requisition approved. Thank you for your help. Goodbye."

Click.

Jose, with his eyes cast down at his budget sheet, shaking his head with a look of dismay on his face, he penciled into the budget one air conditioning system for the Dental Research lab. The rest is history. With one stroke of Jose Coronado's pen, Dr. Shannon's new air conditioning system had made it into the new budget. Jose fulfilled Lupe's request, as promised. And the course of my life had been forever changed.

Though my plans for a summer job at AstroWorld had been dashed, I spent that summer volunteering at the VA Hospital in the Dental Research lab. I did, however, have time to attend a number of Astro's baseball games with my younger cousin, Hollis, and even managed to get in several all-day trips to AstroWorld to boot. More importantly, I had taken my first few steps toward my professional career in dentistry, a career that I would eventually build my entire life around.

Though this series of very fortuitous events sent me on my way to an extremely fulfilling professional career, I often wonder where I would be today if I had gotten my dream job at AstroWorld.

What would I be doing today?

"All aboard! Step right up! Show me your tickets. Welcome to the Texas Cyclone, world's fastest rollercoaster. Watch your step!"

&so;

Two of my childhood friends, Simon and Atilano, noticed my car in the driveway of my mother's house and stopped to lend a helping hand with the moving. Even though we had been close friends as kids, I had seldom crossed paths with Simon over the past few years, and I had seen Atilano even less frequently. I must admit that I was hesitant to impose on my two old friends, but they were intent on helping me load the heavier items into the trailer and would not take "no" for an answer.

After realizing the enormity of the job, I was sure glad they had insisted on offering their assistance. We spent some time chatting, had some laughs, and relived some old memories of our childhood days. We managed to get reacquainted with each other between the loads we were hauling and loading on the trailer.

There was one storage room left to empty before we could call the operation a success, so we began the painstaking task of sorting through the remaining items. At the bottom of a pile in the storage room, we found a painting that my Uncle Neto's wife Barbara had made. It was a collage made from old pieces of driftwood, fish bones, and seashells that she had gathered from the beach at my parent's weekend home in Loyola Beach, near Kingsville, Texas. I hadn't seen this particular piece of artwork in many years, but I could remember it hanging prominently by the fireplace at our beach cottage in Loyola.

17

Just Another Day in Paradise

**Otila Coronado, Arnoldo Cuellar, Pedro Coronado,
Maria Garcia, Guadalupe Cuellar**

Lo-yo-la. The name rolls melodically off the tongue like an old, familiar Bing Crosby melody. Loyola was actually Loyola Beach, Texas, where my father and mother had purchased 2.5 acres of waterfront property on the picturesque shore of Baffin Bay. It lay fifteen miles southeast of Kingsville, Texas. My father Arnoldo had acquired the property at the urging of his brother-in-law, Hollis Young. Since Hollis was an attorney for Mitchell Energy, he loved nothing more than roaming the countryside in search of bargain waterfront property. He enjoyed scouring newspapers and county records in search of reasonably priced land. Hollis and Arnoldo had inspected this property, and Hollis had concluded that it was the perfect parcel of land for Arnoldo and his family. My father must have agreed with Hollis because shortly afterward, he made an offer to the seller, and a deal was struck to buy this piece of waterfront property.

Arnoldo and Lupe's home in Loyola Beach, Texas

Shortly after this purchase, Arnoldo began the backbreaking work of clearing the dense brush from the 2.5 tract of land. Arnoldo was clearly what you might call "old school" when it came to backbreaking work. He could not for a minute fathom the thought of hiring someone to clear the thick brush from the property for him. He was a self-made man, and his pride wouldn't allow him to contract this grueling work out to someone else. He and I spent many torturous weekends with a chainsaw and an axe, clearing mesquite trees and other native shrubs, one by one, from the property until it was manicured to his approval. After the cleanup was finished, he hired Orville Schonenfeld, a local contractor, to build a two-bedroom house with a large family room on the property. In typical Arnoldo fashion, he only wanted the shell of the house built, so he could finish the inside of the house himself.

Within several months the shell of the house had been built, and for the next few months every Friday after work he would pack up his tools, load up the family, and we would head fifty-five miles east to Loyola Beach to finish trimming out the inside of our new weekend home. He and I worked tirelessly on weekends until we finally finished the paneling and trim work on the inside of the house.

Arnoldo couldn't wait for the day when he could host one of those festive Coronado family outings at his new weekend home. For the next fifteen years, until his passing, Loyola would be the site of many Coronado family holiday bashes. Relatives would come to fish, eat Arnoldo's delicious meat off the grill, or just lounge around and take in the beautiful panorama of Baffin Bay from his backyard. Arnoldo loved nothing more than seeing his family enjoying themselves at his weekend home in his personal two and a half acre paradise.

If you had given Arnoldo his choice of 2.5 acres in heaven in exchange for his 2.5 acres in Loyola Beach, I have no doubt he would have responded with something like, "No, thanks. I think I'll just stay right here in Loyola. There's nothing up there that I don't already have down here." This place was undoubtedly his vision of heaven on earth—a place where he was at peace with the world, and he would be content to spend eternity.

Baffin Bay was known for its excellent fishing, and the area immediately in front of Arnoldo's home was one of the best fishing spots on the bay, but there was just one problem: the property didn't have a fishing pier. Being an avid fisherman, he set out to rectify the problem. He promptly petitioned the land commission for a permit to construct a fishing pier and was eventually granted permission to begin construction. He wasted no time starting the project.

The tap-tap-tap of Arnoldo's hammer could be heard around the waterfront neighborhood, as he banged away at the old weather beaten boards. The strange looking contraption he was building stood tall in the backyard. It looked somewhat like an old wooden oil derrick on skis. The tap-tap-tap continued, and it inevitably aroused the curiosity of one of his many colorful neighbors.

"Hey! Arnoldo what are you making?"

Arnoldo looked up to see his neighbor Dr. Kowalski hands on hips, looming in the shadows behind him. Dr. Kowalski or just plain "Kowalski" as Arnoldo called him, was a mathematics professor at Texas A&I University in Kingsville. Kowalski also had a weekend home, just down the street from Arnoldo's. He was a good neighbor and a nice fellow, but he was one of those nosy, "know it all" types that seemed to delight in criticizing other people's ideas. Kowalski was not the least bit bashful about sharing his annoying, unsolicited advice with anyone who would listen. Arnoldo already knew what would be coming out of Kowalski's mouth next, but being the ever-cordial neighbor that he was, he politely decided to answer Kowalski's query.

"I'm building a platform so that I can drive 4x4 pilings into the bottom of the bay for the new fishing pier I'm planning to build." He looked up at Kowalski, smiled and kept tapping with his hammer.

"Arnoldo, you need to call Tony Schmitt. He's got a water jet contraption that can set those posts in one afternoon. He set the posts on my pier, and it only cost me three hundred and fifty dollars. Look how straight my pier is. That rickety thing you're making will never work."

Well, this idea didn't interest Arnoldo in the least because he thought that three hundred and fifty dollars was an obscene amount to pay for a job that he could accomplish with some old fashioned ingenuity. He had already salvaged some nails and boards from remnants of an old pier that a storm had washed up on his beach, and that was all he needed. He knew that this particular project wasn't going to be easy, but now that Kowalski had ridiculed his invention and wounded his pride, it had become a personal challenge to him. He was now more determined than ever to build the contraption, just to prove Kowalski wrong.

He glanced up at Kowalski and said, "You're probably right that it won't work, but I needed to use up these old boards, and I've already started, so I'm going to finish it anyway."

"You're wasting your time, Arnoldo. I'll keep Tony's number for you when you decide to quit being so hard headed." Kowalski stormed back toward his house, shaking his head and grumbling to himself because his advice had fallen on deaf ears. Arnoldo, undeterred, kept on with his tap-tap-tap.

By the end of the weekend, Arnoldo had built a towering platform on skids, which he had placed prominently beside his house to make sure Kowalski could see it from his backyard. On the inside of the platform, suspended by a system of pulleys, was a large airplane engine piston that he had bought at a salvage yard. This large piston was to be raised and dropped on the 4x4 posts until they were driven deep into the sand at the bottom of the bay. The skids allowed him to slide the contraption as he drove pilings further into the bay. These pilings would eventually support the entire structure of the pier.

By this time I was off at college, so Arnoldo didn't have anyone to assist him with the building of the pier. This was no problem for him because he had designed this device to be operated by a single person. Over the next few weeks, the neighborhood was filled with pounding sounds of wooden pilings caused by this remarkable contraption he had designed and built himself.

Within a couple of months, Arnoldo had methodically driven in all the support pilings and had constructed the entire pier. Finally, he could be seen sitting at the end of his newly built fishing pier sipping coffee from his mug, beaming with pride over his accomplishment.

Kowalski was nowhere to be seen for several weeks. When he finally came back around, he just couldn't help himself.

"Arnoldo, this pier would have been a lot straighter if you had done it the way I told you to do it."

Arnoldo just smiled, content in knowing that he had proven Kowalski wrong. He also accepted the fact that Kowalski would never admit that he had been mistaken about Arnoldo's homemade contraption. So Arnoldo shrugged it off, and they remained good friends and neighbors for many years.

My dad's other big battle was the one he waged with the sea. He had noticed that the spring high tides had started to erode much of the shoreline on his end of Baffin Bay. He had paid good money for this property, and by God, he took it very personally that the sea was robbing him of his land, a little bit at a time. He had decided that it was high time he did something about it. He had found an old cement mixer with no motor and repaired it with a motor he had salvaged from and old electric lawn mower. With a little work and some ingenuity, he now had a fully operational cement mixer. Knowing that he had an endless supply of sand on the beach, he decided to combine some of this sand with bags of concrete in his cement mixer to make large cement blocks.

From these blocks, he would build a bulkhead. This concrete structure would serve as a sea wall to protect his property from further erosion by the high tides. He had constructed some wooden forms in which to pour the concrete and manufactured about fifty cement blocks about two feet tall by three feet wide, each one weighing nearly a hundred pounds. Like the Egyptians, patiently and methodically building the pyramids, we dragged each block into place and assembled the wall that ran the entire length of the property over a period of about a year.

Arnoldo was somewhat obsessed with this project. He could be seen shoveling sand and pouring concrete almost every weekend for the better part of a year until the project was completed.

Kowalski had been by several times and reassured Arnoldo that he was wasting his time trying to fight the sea, but Arnoldo was used to Kowalski's nay saying and never let this kind of talk deter him from completing his projects. As usual, he shrugged off Kowalski's advice and went on with his project.

Within five years of completion, Arnoldo's shoreline had remained exactly where it had been when he purchased it. And now, his property jutted out like a peninsula because all of his adjoining neighbors, including Kowalski, had lost 20 to 30 ft. of their shoreline to erosion. Arnoldo had successfully fought the sea to a draw, and always beamed with pride when anyone admired his sea wall. He faithfully maintained and repaired the sea wall until the day he died in 1985.

I can't help but wonder sometimes what the conversation might have been when Arnoldo reached St. Peter's Pearly Gates. Did he get his choice between the 2.5 acres in heaven or the 2.5 acres at Loyola Beach? If he did, I suspect I know just where his spirit resides today, because he most certainly would have said, "No thanks, I think I'll stay right here in Loyola."

My father Arnoldo passed away in 1985, and Loyola just wasn't the same without him. He had been the one breathing life into that 2.5 acre parcel of land, and somehow it just seemed gaunt and lifeless without him. I struggled to keep it groomed and mowed as well as he had lovingly managed to do for so many years. Lupe, my mother, had not returned but once or twice since he died because Loyola had lost all of its luster and charm without Arnoldo at her side. Though she knew that she could never recapture the almost magical exhilaration and happiness that had once been the essence of Loyola, she couldn't bear the thought of parting with this precious ground that my father loved so much. So, I did my very best to maintain it as best I could for her.

18

Of Garden Tractor Repair
and Roadside Despair

My father Arnoldo had an old International Harvester Cub Cadet garden tractor that he had used to mow his 2.5 acres at Loyola for many years, and I had helped him repair it many times. It was a very durable piece of equipment that took all the abuse that this rugged parcel of land had to offer. Arnoldo had managed to keep the tractor in good repair by refurbishing or manufacturing his own replacement parts, as there was not an International Harvester dealer in the area. I had been using this tractor to mow this acreage for the past year, and I managed to repair it each time it had broken down. But this last time there was a more serious mechanical problem that I hadn't been able to fix myself. After considering my options, I decided to seek assistance from the best shade tree mechanic I knew, my Uncle Ernesto Coronado.

International Harvester Cub Cadet

Since Ernesto's father Pedro had been an automobile mechanic much of his life, it wasn't so surprising that Neto had inherited an obsession for high-performance cars. He had learned much about auto repair from his father, and now that he had gone to work for the VA Hospital, he was earning money and had the itch for a nice automobile. Knowing that he couldn't afford a newer upscale car, he decided to buy a used Mercedes Benz. He found just the one he wanted, at the right price, and proceeded to buy it and restore it to showroom condition. He spent countless hours under the hood of this car, cleaning the engine and restoring it to mint condition. Every piece of chrome was polished to perfection, and the body was detailed to a high luster. It was his pride and joy, and he never missed an opportunity to pop open the hood and show you his perfectly tuned, spotless engine.

It was my Uncle Neto's kind and generous nature, along with his mechanical background, that led me to call on him when I needed help repairing my father's old garden tractor. He had helped me once before with some minor repairs but could not resist poking fun at my cheap tools that had been made in Taiwan. He was a connoisseur of quality mechanic's tools, and I had to listen to this story about my cheap, Taiwanese tools every time we had a family gathering. This time I was prepared.

I had just started my dental practice and one of my patients worked for Snap On Tools, a high quality tool manufacturer. My patient needed new teeth, and I was in need of some better tools, so a deal was struck, and I had acquired a new set of quality tools to show my uncle next time I got a chance. Maybe he would quit telling the story about my cheap Taiwanese tools now. I called him, and he offered to come by the following weekend to help me repair the broken garden tractor.

We met at my mother's house in Benavides, where we planned to load the broken tractor on a trailer and haul it to Loyola for repair. We would leave it there after repairs were done for use on future mowing. The plan had one minor flaw, though. My car didn't have a trailer hitch, and I wouldn't dream of asking my Uncle Neto to hitch a trailer to his shiny, newly restored Mercedes.

Fortunately for us, my friend Simon had an old "junker" of a pick- up truck, and he offered to let us borrow it for the weekend so that we could transport the trailer and tractor to Loyola. I am not dealing in hyperbole when I refer to this pick up as a junker. You could count the white stripes on the highway from the 10 inch, rusted hole in the floorboard beneath the gas pedal. This was only one of numerous holes, which provided more than adequate ventilation while driving down the highway. The problem came when the engine idled. If the truck wasn't moving, the cab would fill up with carbon monoxide fumes from the exhaust. Also because of the road noise caused by the holes in the floor, you had to yell to the other passenger to be heard. Oh well, these were only minor inconveniences that we could easily overcome.

Simon's pick-up truck

Against my Uncle Neto's better judgment, we loaded the tractor on the trailer and hitched it up to the old pick-up. I had finally succeeded in convincing him that this old pick up was reliable enough to get us where we needed to go, a decision we would both come to regret in the near future. Being the knowledgeable mechanic that he was, his instincts told him that this truck was an accident looking for a place to happen, but he bit his tongue and climbed into the cab with me.

We headed 55 miles east to Loyola. To my uncle's surprise, the truck, trailer, and both of us arrived in one piece, with no problems. "I knew this old pick up would get us here," I said to Neto, with a sheepish smile. He just shook his head and muttered prophetically, "We're not home yet."

Neto set up the workspace in the garage like a surgical operatory. Tools were placed in strategic places, and the tractor was positioned in the center on a work platform, like a patient laying on the operating table. Every tool was ready, and all our supplies were laid out. The tractor was prepared for surgery. We spent that evening, and most of the next day taking that tractor apart, bolt by bolt. Every grease fitting was filled with grease, the carburetor was taken apart and cleaned, belts and pulleys were cleaned replaced with parts that my father had kept on hand for emergencies. By Saturday afternoon, we had refurbished the tractor, and it was running like a top. When we finished we both had a beer to celebrate our accomplishment. Our mission having been accomplished, we decided to load up the old pick-up and head for home.

We were both covered in grease from head to toe. Our clothes, our hands and our faces were black with grit. We both agreed that we would not take a shower at the house in Loyola because we would probably clog up the drain with grease and oil. Our plan was to get ourselves back to Benavides where we could get a bar of soap, shed our greasy clothes, and scrub some of the grease off of ourselves in the backyard, before we showered inside. No one would see us in this condition before we got home anyway, so we climbed in the truck and contentedly headed back to Benavides.

We had just gotten on Highway 77, about 12 miles from Kingsville, when the truck engine began to sputter. I looked at Neto, and he looked at me with a pained expression on his face. I knew that look. It spoke volumes to me. It said, I knew I shouldn't have let you talk me into driving this piece of junk. I silently prayed that the truck motor would stop coughing and sputtering, because I knew I was on the verge of becoming the subject of one of the comical stories my Uncle Neto was so famous for. Call it fate, failure to heed warning signs, bad planning, or just plain bad luck, but the truck limped to a stop and the motor died.

It didn't take Uncle Neto but a few minutes and a few choice expletives to diagnose that the points on the engine were completely worn, and would need replacing. This would have been fine if we were in town or near a phone, but we were broken down on State Highway 77, twelve miles from the nearest civilization.

We tried, but soon found that there was no hope of restarting the engine. It was late afternoon, and our only hope was to hitch a ride into town to get Paul Corkill, Jr., who lived in nearby Kingsville. He could tow us into town for repairs. Now, all that remained was for us to thumb a ride into town.

This seemed easy enough until it dawned on us how awful we looked. We were covered in oil and grease, marooned by the side of the road with this rusted out clunker of a pick-up. We stuck out greasy thumbs to solicit a ride, but cars would slow down, take one look at us and speed up again. It became quite apparent to us that no one wanted to let us inside their cars because of our grimy looks. Frankly, I couldn't blame them, either. Neto, always the one to find the humor in an utterly frustrating situation, began waving his Mercedes car key in the air and shouting, "I'm not a bum. I own a Mercedes!"

We both sat on the tailgate of the truck and laughed until our stomachs hurt. Neto's sense of humor somehow had made this utterly pathetic situation we were in seem hysterically funny. After about 30 futile minutes of attempting to hitch a ride, an old farmer in a pickup truck stopped, took pity on us and gave us a ride into town in the bed of his truck, where we were able to get help and return to Benavides.

Despite all the minor glitches, it had been a very fruitful trip. The tractor had been fixed, and I would be able to continue to mow the grass at Loyola with my father's trusty old tractor. It was a small achievement, but a significant one, nonetheless, as it was my small way of helping Loyola live on.

When I remember people from my past, especially my relatives, I usually picture them doing what they loved best, in the places they loved the most. For instance, I imagine Ma Tila, my grandmother, sitting on her front porch swinging back and forth on her glider chair while watching the hummingbirds in her flowerbeds and praying her daily rosary. "Dios te salve, Maria, llena eres de gracia, el Senor es con tigo. Bendita tu eres entre todas las mujeres...."

I can see my grandfather, Pedro Coronado, sitting on his metal stool behind the counter of Coronado's Garage, exchanging colorful tall tales with his old cronies. I picture my Uncle Ernesto, with his head under the hood of his car, tuning up the engine with a socket wrench in one hand and a red, oily rag in the other. As for Arnoldo, my father, it is pretty easy. I picture him in his khaki colored pants and white t-shirt, grilling his favorite cuts of meat on the pit, surrounded by friends and family at Loyola.

଼

Jan positioned herself at the back door, holding it wide open as Simon, Atilano and I guided the big metal filing cabinet from the storage room through the living room and out to the driveway where the trailer awaited. With a mighty heave and a few groans, the three of us hoisted the metal cabinet onto the last remaining space on the already tightly packed utility trailer. Jan and I looked at each other in near disbelief. We could hardly believe it. Could it be that we had finally succeeded in the monumental task of emptying the contents of the entire house.

We had successfully boxed up and carted off a lifetime of my memories. This would be the last trip. You might think that the finality of emptying ones childhood home of its contents would foster feelings of sadness. In truth, it was a bit unsettling to witness bits and pieces of my boyhood home being packaged into cardboard boxes and carried away, leaving an empty shell in their wake. In a larger sense, however, I had gained a new perspective on my life, which had brought me a comforting sense of inner peace.

That morning, I had started my journey to Benavides with an unsettling feeling of loss, because I knew that I was severing the last ties to my hometown and ultimately, to that part of my life. This parting of ways with my family home afforded me the opportunity to relive memories of the people and places that served to mold me into the adult I am. These memories and the experiences derived from them have shaped my character, and to this day continue to define the person that I am. I have found great solace in the realization that, though my life's journey has led me down many a distant, twisting and winding highway, it seems that, in the end, all roads have led me home.

By day's end, I had come to understand more clearly how people and places like Coronado's Garage, which I thought I was leaving behind, had actually become an integral part of the life I enjoyed in the present. I was reminded of a quote from one of my favorite authors, Garrison Keillor, who said that "the good things in life are like snowflakes. You can hold them briefly, and they can bring much joy to your life, but you cannot keep them forever." While Mr. Keillor's assertion may hold true in the shadow of my material possessions, it most certainly does not apply to my most precious possessions of all—my memories.

You see, I now understand that I am Coronado's Garage.

Proof

Made in the USA
Charleston, SC
24 February 2014